REVISE BTEC NATIONAL
Children's Play, Learning and Development
REVISION GUIDE

Series Consultant: Harry Smith

Author: Brenda Baker

Unit 4 research structure: Georgina Shaw

A note from the publisher

Published by Pearson Education Limited, 80 Strand, London, WC2R 0RL.

www.pearsonschoolsandfecolleges.co.uk

Copies of official specifications for all Pearson qualifications may be found on the website: qualifications.pearson.com

Text and illustrations © Pearson Education Limited 2017
Typeset and illustrated by Kamae Design, Oxford
Produced by Out of House Publishing
Cover illustration by Miriam Sturdee

The right of Brenda Baker to be identified as author of this work has been asserted by her in accordance with the Copyright, Designs and Patents Act 1988.

First published 2017

20 19 18 17
10 9 8 7 6 5 4 3 2 1

British Library Cataloguing in Publication Data
A catalogue record for this book is available from the British Library

ISBN 978 1 292 23047 4

Printed in Slovakia by Neografia

Acknowledgements

We are grateful to the following for permission to reproduce copyright material:

Text
Extract on page 124, 136,137,138 from SAMTAB (source, appearance, method, timeliness, applicability, balance) - method for completion for assessing suitability of sources © Georgina Shaw, with permission; Link on page 139 from Provision for Learning Outdoors for Under 5s, State of the Nation survey, Final Report February 2016,Early Childhood Forum, used with permission; Link on page 139 from The Effective Provision Of Pre-School Education (EPPE) Project, Institute of Education with permission.

The publisher would like to thank the following for their kind permission to reproduce their photographs:

(Key: b-bottom; c-centre; l-left; r-right; t-top)

123RF.com: 104, Sergiy Bykhunenko 13; **Alamy Images:** Angela Hampton Picture Library 24tl, BRU News 22, BSIP SA 108, Buzzshotz 33c, christopher jones 86, Cultura Creative (RF) 3bl, Cultura RM 51, Gary Roebuck 56, Judith Collins 76tr, Kumar Sriskandan 132, Mark Richardson 83, Marmaduke St. John 103, moodboard 9r, Picture Partners 8cr, Sally and Richard Greenhill 63, veryan dale 74c, 74b; **Brenda Baker:** 74t; **Fotolia.com:** Click Images 9l, Kevin Mayer 2l, micromonkey 27b, Monkey Business 33b, nadezhda1906 28, nd3000 82, Oksana Kuzmina 35tr, WavebreakmediaMicro 33t, ziggy 8tr; **Getty Images:** amana productions inc. 76br, Blend Images - JGI / Jamie Grill 3cl, Brian MitchellI 27c, Chris Schmidt 99, Christopher Futcher 100, Compassionate Eye Foundation / Inti St. Clair 27t, Daniel Grill 54, Dann Tardif 18b, David Woolfall 8tl, DGLimages 111, Djordje Zoric 8cl, 31, Hero Images 29, 76bl, IAN HOOTON / SPL 15tr, Jamie Grill 15br, Jodi Jacobson 15bl, joecicak 134, Judith Haeusler 24bl, KidStock 16, Kreg Holt 1l, Mike Kemp 1r, Miodrag Gajic 81, Peter Cade 18t, PhotoAlto / Anne-Sophie Bost 18c, PhotoAlto / Sandro Di Carlo Darsa 49tl, shorrocks 87, Stockbyte 76tl, Vanessa Davies 2r, 15bc; **Pearson Education Ltd:** Studio 8 3br, 15tc, 49tr, 49bl, 49br, Lord and Leverett 35br, 57, 128, Jules Selmes 3t, 3cr, 14, 19, 35l, 59, 60t, 60b, 69, 70, 73, 98, 110, 113; **Photolibrary.com:** SW Productions / White 130; **Shutterstock.com:** Andrey Stratilatov 71, Beneda Miroslav 1c, Capifrutta 58, Denis Kuvaev 7, jannoon028 106, Mastering_Microstock 2c, Olesya Feketa 131, StockLite 15tl, Tyler Olson 11, 80, wavebreakmedia 123

All other images © Pearson Education

Notes from the publisher

1.

In order to ensure that this resource offers high-quality support for the associated Pearson qualification, it has been through a review process by the awarding body. This process confirms that this resource fully covers the teaching and learning content of the specification or part of a specification at which it is aimed. It also confirms that it demonstrates an appropriate balance between the development of subject skills, knowledge and understanding, in addition to preparation for assessment.

Endorsement does not cover any guidance on assessment activities or processes (e.g. practice questions or advice on how to answer assessment questions), included in the resource nor does it prescribe any particular approach to the teaching or delivery of a related course.

While the publishers have made every attempt to ensure that advice on the qualification and its assessment is accurate, the official specification and associated assessment guidance materials are the only authoritative source of information and should always be referred to for definitive guidance.

Pearson examiners have not contributed to any sections in this resource relevant to examination papers for which they have responsibility.

Examiners will not use endorsed resources as a source of material for any assessment set by Pearson.

Endorsement of a resource does not mean that the resource is required to achieve this Pearson qualification, nor does it mean that it is the only suitable material available to support the qualification, and any resource lists produced by the awarding body shall include this and other appropriate resources.

2.

Pearson has robust editorial processes, including answer and fact checks, to ensure the accuracy of the content in this publication, and every effort is made to ensure this publication is free of errors. We are, however, only human, and occasionally errors do occur. Pearson is not liable for any misunderstandings that arise as a result of errors in this publication, but it is our priority to ensure that the content is accurate. If you spot an error, please do contact us at resourcescorrections@pearson.com so we can make sure it is corrected.

Websites
Pearson Education Limited is not responsible for the content of any external internet sites. It is essential for tutors to preview each website before using it in class so as to ensure that the URL is still accurate, relevant and appropriate. We suggest that tutors bookmark useful websites and consider enabling students to access them through the school/college intranet.

Introduction

Which units should you revise?

This Revision Guide has been designed to support you in preparing for the externally assessed units of your course. Remember that you won't necessarily be studying all the units included here – it will depend on the qualification you are taking.

BTEC National Qualification	Externally assessed units
For each of the following: Extended Certificate Foundation Diploma Diploma	1 Children's Development 2 Development of Children's Communication, Literacy and Numeracy Skills
Extended Diploma	1 Children's Development 2 Development of Children's Communication, Literacy and Numeracy Skills 4 Enquiries into Current Research in Early Years Practice

Your Revision Guide

Each unit in this Revision Guide contains two types of pages, shown below.v

Content **pages** help you revise the essential content you need to know for each unit.

Skills **pages** help you prepare for your exam or assessed task. Skills pages have a coloured edge and are shaded in the table of contents.

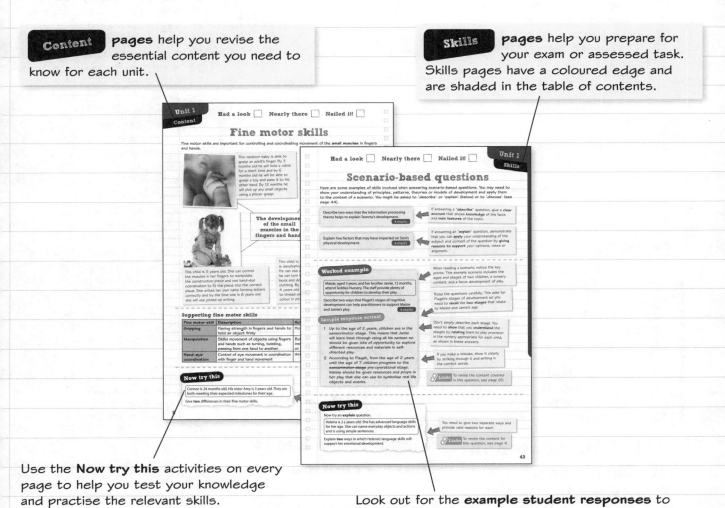

Use the **Now try this** activities on every page to help you test your knowledge and practise the relevant skills.

Look out for the **example student responses** to revision questions or tasks on the skills pages. Post-its will explain their strengths and weaknesses.

Contents

A small bit of small print
Pearson publishes Sample Assessment Material and the Specification on its website. This is the official content and this book should be used in conjunction with it. The questions in *Now try this* have been written to help you test your knowledge and skills. Remember: the real assessment may not look like this.

Growth

Growth is sometimes referred to as physiological change. It describes an increase in length, height, weight and body dimensions.

Principles of growth

As children grow, they begin to develop coordination and balance, and gain control of their muscles.

- Growth rates are not continuous. Periods of more rapid growth are called **growth spurts**.
- Different parts of the body grow at different rates.
- Rates of growth vary between children of the same age.
- Rates of growth vary between boys and girls.

Recording growth

Length or **height**, **head circumference** and **weight** are plotted on a growth chart called a **centile chart**. Growth charts have been developed using statistics from a large number of children to find 'norms' of growth in each age group.

- Growth is a measure of children's health and well-being.
- Comparing growth against norms is important to identify signs of ill health and problems in development.
- Growth charts tell you how big or heavy children are expected to be at a certain age.
- Growth charts are different for boys and girls as their expected rate of growth varies.

Measuring growth

Head circumference

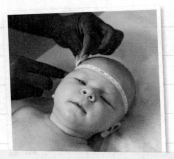

Measurement is taken across the forehead: just above the ears and at the midpoint of the back of the head.

Weight

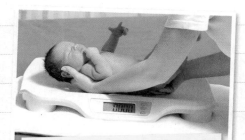

Babies should be weighed by laying them in a special baby scale until around 2 years old, when they can stand alone on a digital scale.

Height

Children grow rapidly and will reach very roughly half their adult height by the time they are 2 years old.

Skull growth

✓ This is measured at **birth** and between **6 and 8 weeks** to identify any abnormality in brain/skull growth. Skull growth occurs faster in the first 2 years of life but continues up to early adulthood.

Weight increase

✓ Children will **triple** their birth weight by the time they are **12 months old**.

Length or height?

✓ In the first 2 years, an infant's **length** is measured when lying down.

✓ From 2 years old, their **height** is measured when standing.

Now try this

Baby Brad is 8 weeks old. The health visitor is checking his weight. She will plot it on a centile chart.

Identify **two** other measurements that the health visitor will take.

Development

Development describes the acquisition of skills and abilities through a life stage.

Principles of development

Development follows an orderly sequence. Each stage in the sequence is called a **milestone**.

- The rate of development varies between children of the same age.
- Physical development starts with control of the head down the body: '**head to toe**'.
- Physical development starts with larger movements and gradually becomes more refined as children gain control of smaller muscles: '**inner to outer**'.
- Various factors can affect the rate of development.

Factors affecting development

Development can be affected by five key factors.

1 Growth

2 Genetics

3 The environment

4 Stimulation

5 Illness or injury

Areas of development

Development takes place in four key areas.

Development is holistic but each area of development is interrelated.

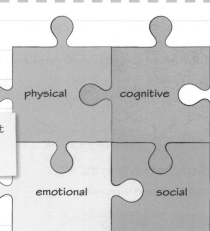

physical   cognitive

emotional   social

Physical development: head to toe

1 Physical development starts with simple reflexes followed by control of head movement.

2 Control moves down the shoulders and back enabling children to sit unaided.

3 Control continues down the trunk to the legs and feet to enable children to crawl, stand and walk.

Now try this

The children in the photos above are each meeting their expected milestones. Identify the approximate age of each child.

Areas of development

Development is **holistic**. You need to understand each different area of development as well as how these can impact on each other. There are five key areas of development.

Physical – how children acquire large movements such as locomotion, movement, balance and coordination, and fine movements of the fingers and hands including hand–eye coordination.

Cognitive – the development of intellectual ability, memory and thinking skills, problem solving and understanding.

Areas of development

Language – the development of verbal and non-verbal forms of communication.

Emotional – the development of self-concept, self-esteem and confidence; the ability to express and cope with feelings about themselves and others.

Social – the ability to relate to others, form attachments and relationships with adults, and develop friendships with other children.

Now try this

Emma is 4 years old and still very dependent on her mother. She often becomes frustrated and has temper tantrums.

Which area of her development is affected?

Holistic development

Holistic development describes the interrelationships between areas of development. However, children may not develop at the same rate in every area of their development.

Interrelationships

Areas of development are dependent on, and influence, each other.

👍 Advanced development in one area can enhance development in one or more areas of development.

👎 A delay in one area of development can impact negatively on one or more other areas.

- -

Here are some ways that each area of development is related to others.

Physical: gross motor
Important for:
- physical growth and abilities that can impact on how children join in with physical games that enable them to socialise with friends
- physical activity to help children to gain a sense of achievement that helps to build self-esteem.

Physical: fine motor
Important for:
- children to explore and manipulate materials; to construct and develop concepts
- handwriting skills for the development of communication and language
- independence in personal care leading to self-esteem.

Cognitive
Important for:
- the development of language
- negotiating and cooperating in social play
- children to understand and express their feelings, which helps to promote emotional development.

Language
Important for:
- children to be able to express their feelings in order to be able to cope with emotions
- supporting their thought processes
- socialising and building effective friendships.

Social
Important for:
- building relationships with adults that can support children's speech and language, and develop their thinking skills
- effective friendships that can have positive effects on self-concept and build high self-esteem
- confidence and willingness to join in with physical activities and games that are needed for physical development.

Emotional
Important for:
- a positive self-image
- confidence in order to try out new activities that will support physical and cognitive development
- developing secure attachments that promote effective interaction with parents and carers
- developing positive self-esteem, which helps in the development of friendships.

- -

Now try this

> Joseph is 4 years old. He has just joined the reception class. Joseph has language delay.

Suggest how Joseph's language delay may have an impact on his cognitive, social and emotional development. Give one way relating to each area.

Neurological development

Neurological development (brain development) describes the growth of the brain and the forming of new neurological connections.

Early development

The first few years of life are the most critical time for brain development. The development of the brain is influenced by:

- a predisposition inherited from a parent
- experiences.

> 🔗 **Links** Look at page 11 to revise the influences of nature and nurture.

Neurons

Neurons are single brain cells. There are billions of neurons in the brain. Electrical signals are sent and received between neurons. These are important for an individual's thought processes and actions.

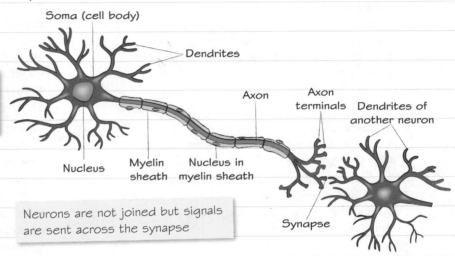

Soma (cell body)
Dendrites
Axon
Axon terminals
Dendrites of another neuron
Nucleus
Myelin sheath
Nucleus in myelin sheath
Synapse

> Neurons are not joined but signals are sent across the synapse

Neural pathways

Connections between neurons are called **neural pathways**. They help information to move more easily.

- There are already neural pathways in the brain at birth.
- Experiences develop more neural pathways.
- Neural pathways that are not used are removed. This begins at around 18 months of age.

Periods of neurological development

There are critical periods for the development of different parts of the brain in the child's early years. It starts with the development of the senses.

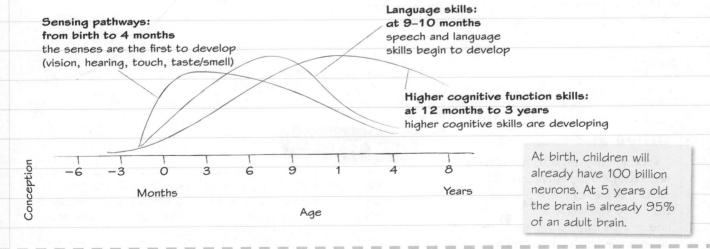

Sensing pathways:
from birth to 4 months
the senses are the first to develop
(vision, hearing, touch, taste/smell)

Language skills:
at 9–10 months
speech and language skills begin to develop

Higher cognitive function skills:
at 12 months to 3 years
higher cognitive skills are developing

Conception

−6   −3   0   3   6   9   1   4   8

Months   Years

Age

> At birth, children will already have 100 billion neurons. At 5 years old the brain is already 95% of an adult brain.

> **Now try this**

Give **two** reasons why it is important to engage with babies and young children for neurological development.

Atypical development

Atypical development describes development that does not follow the expected patterns.

Types

You need to recognise these four different types of atypical development.

 Delayed global development
The child's development is delayed across all areas of development.

Example: A child who is 5 years old is meeting the milestones that are expected for a 4-year-old in physical, cognitive, language, emotional and social development.

 Specific delay
A child's development is delayed in one area or aspect of their development.

Example: A child who is meeting the expected milestones in physical, cognitive, language and social development but is emotionally insecure.

 Gifted
The child's cognitive and language development is more advanced than expected for their age.

Example: A child who is frequently asking questions, has a wider vocabulary than others at the same age, is reasoning, understanding abstract concepts at an early age, and is displaying higher level thinking.

 Talented
A child has skills and abilities that are advanced for their age, such as in their physical development or musical or artistic abilities.

Example: A child who has learned to play an instrument at an early age, is a skilled gymnast, or whose paintings or drawings show a level of skill that is unusual for their age.

To provide support at an early stage

To reduce the impact on other areas of development

The importance of recognising atypical development

To refer to appropriate specialist support

To involve and work with parents

To reduce the impact on behaviour

Gifted and talented

Although children who are gifted and talented are advanced in certain areas of development, they may also have additional needs that should be recognised at an early stage. Not having their needs met may lead to social and emotional problems such as low self-esteem or difficulties in forming friendships.

Now try this

Manju is 4 years old. He is meeting his expected milestones in most areas of development but is having difficulty with his speech. His key person at nursery, and other children, find him difficult to understand as his pronunciation is not clear.

1 Identify the type of atypical development Manju is exhibiting.
2 Give **three** examples of how Manju's speech difficulty may impact on his emotional and social development.

Genetic inheritance

Heredity defines the nature of individuals. Genes are sets of instructions to the cells that determine growth and development. Individuals inherit 23 pairs of chromosomes that contain genes from each parent.

Inherited genes

Although the genes a child inherits from their parents determine certain traits and predispositions, other factors determine how they are shaped and expressed.

- **Genotype** is the genetic information that a child inherits from their parents.
- **Phenotype** refers to the way the genes are expressed in the characteristics of the child.

Physical traits

These include characteristics such as **height**, **skin pigmentation** and **eye colour**, which are all determined by **genes**. Because a child inherits genes from both mother and father, the way in which they are expressed depends on the interaction of these genes. A child may inherit a gene for blue eyes from their mother and brown eyes from their father but they are likely to have brown eyes because the brown eye gene is dominant.

Psychological traits

These include being skilled in mathematics, being creative, or being extrovert or introvert. A child may have a predisposition to be creative because of the genes they inherit but they would need a suitable environment for their creativity to be expressed.

Genetic conditions

Health conditions can arise from defective inherited genes.

Dominant genes

A **defective gene** can be passed on from **one parent or both**. The likelihood of developing a condition depends upon whether the defective gene is recessive or dominant. A **dominant gene** needs only to be passed on by one parent for the child to develop a condition, for example:

- **brittle bone disease** – causes bones to break easily
- **Huntington's disease** – causes involuntary movement, cognitive and psychiatric disorders.

Recessive genes

A **recessive gene** must be passed on from **both parents** for the child to develop the condition. For example:

- **cystic fibrosis** – causes a build-up of thick, sticky mucus that can damage the body's organs
- **phenylketonuria (PKU)** – can lead to intellectual disability and developmental delay
- **Duchenne muscular dystrophy** – causes muscle weakness and wasting, and the resulting difficulty with motor skills and walking.

If the defective gene is passed from one parent only, the child becomes a **carrier**.

Abnormality of chromosomes: individuals with Down's syndrome have an extra copy of chromosome 21. It causes characteristic facial features, growth delay and intellectual disability.

Now try this

Identify:

(a) **two** physical traits that can be inherited from parents

(b) **two** psychological traits that may be inherited from parents.

Fine motor skills

Fine motor skills are important for controlling and coordinating movement of the **small muscles** in fingers and hands.

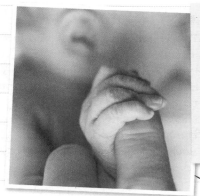

This newborn baby is able to grasp an adult's finger. By 3 months old he will hold a rattle for a short time and by 6 months old he will be able to grasp a toy and pass it to his other hand. By 12 months he will pick up any small objects using a pincer grasp.

The development of the small muscles in the fingers and hands

This child is 18 months old. She can build with small blocks, use a spoon and make marks with crayons using a palmer grasp. When she reaches 2 years old she will be able to pull on her shoes and control her crayon to draw circles and dots.

This child is 5 years old. She can control the muscles in her fingers to manipulate the construction piece and use hand–eye coordination to fit the piece into the correct place. She writes her own name forming letters correctly and by the time she is 8 years old she will use joined-up writing.

This child is 3 years old. He is developing a tripod grasp. He can use a fork and spoon, he can turn the pages of a book and do up and unbutton clothing. By the time he is 4 years old he will be able to thread small beads and colour in pictures.

Supporting fine motor skills

Fine motor skill	Description	Activity to support and promote this skill
Gripping	Having strength in fingers and hands to hold an object firmly	Holding a rattle, tricycle handle or spoon
Manipulation	Skilful movement of objects using fingers and hands such as turning, twisting, passing from one hand to another	Building with blocks, playing a musical instrument, playing and placing farm animals or cars
Hand–eye coordination	Control of eye movement in coordination with finger and hand movement	Writing, sewing, doing jigsaw puzzles

Now try this

Connor is 24 months old. His sister Amy is 3 years old. They are both meeting their expected milestones for their age.

Give **two** differences in their fine motor skills.

You must make sure that you make links between the children described in the case study and the developmental milestones expected at their age.

Gross motor skills

Gross motor skills allow children to control the **large muscles** in their torso, arms, legs, hands and feet.

Infancy: 0–2 years

Age	Gross motor skill	The impact on development
3 months	Lifts up chest and head when lying on front; moves arms together	Once babies begin to move independently they can interact with their environment. Movement will strengthen bones and muscles. They begin to coordinate movement to enable them to reach out to investigate toys and other objects.
6 months	Can sit with support; rolls over from front to back and back to front	
9 months	Sits unaided; crawls	
12 months	Stands alone; walks by holding on	Becoming increasingly mobile helps young children to explore more of their environment. This encourages their inquisitiveness, leading to new ideas and the development of concepts. Developing greater strength in large muscles supports physical play, balance and coordination of movement.
15 months	Crawls up steps; walks	
18 months	Squats, walks up steps with help; can climb on to low object	
2 years	Runs; propels sit-on toy; climbs on to low furniture	

Early childhood: 3–8 years

From about 3–4 years old children can balance and walk along a line. From around 5–8 years old they can balance on a low beam.

From about 3–4 years old children can hop on one foot. By around 5–8 years old they can hop, skip and jump with confidence.

From about 3–4 years old children can run forwards and backwards. From around 5–8 years old they can skip with a rope.

Children continue to develop gross motor skills

From about 3 years old most children can throw a ball and by around 4 years old can aim it. At approximately 5–8 years old they can throw a ball accurately and catch it.

From about 3 years old children can pedal and control a tricycle. From around 6 years old they can ride a bicycle.

Now try this

Give **three** reasons why physical development, including gross and fine motor skills, is important to children's social play.

 **Links** Look at pages 4 and 8 to help you.

Maslow

Abraham Maslow was a psychologist who studied the needs of individuals to help them to achieve personal fulfilment. He came to the conclusion that basic needs must be met before moving to higher level needs. In 1943 he developed a theoretical model, referred to as **Maslow's hierarchy of needs**.

Maslow's hierarchy of needs

Self-actualisation — Self-fulfilment through mental stimulation

Self-esteem — Self-worth and sense of identity

Social needs — Social interaction, love and affection

Safety and security — A need to feel safe and protected from danger

Physiological needs — Basic needs for survival: air, food, water, shelter, warmth, clothing, sleep

Needs

Maslow viewed the first four stages as **basic needs**. These need to be satisfied before being able to become personally fulfilled.

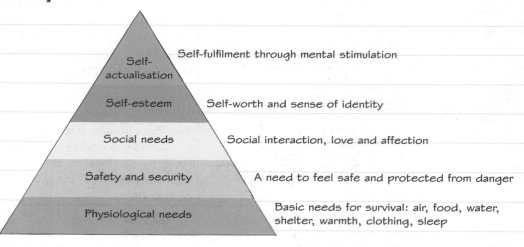

5 Meeting children's needs at each of the four stages provides the foundation that children need to be able to reach their full potential.

3 Children need love and affection. This helps them to develop a sense of belonging, without which they may feel isolated. Children who feel loved are more able to develop effective friendships and relationships, and cope with life events.

4 At around 20 months young children develop a sense of self. Respecting children's individuality and encouraging independence helps to foster positive self-esteem and confidence.

1 Meeting children's physiological needs is also critical for physical and brain growth, and health. In practice, this means providing a nutritious diet, a warm, safe home and clothing that is adequate for the weather.

2 Children need to feel safe and secure. This means being protected from harm and abuse, having familiar routines and addressing their health needs.

Now try this

Aimee is 3 years old and she is due to begin nursery. A key person has been identified who will be the first point of contact for Aimee and her parents.

Give **three** reasons why the key person role is important for ensuring that Aimee's needs are being met with reference to Maslow's hierarchy of needs.

Nature versus nurture

It is widely accepted that human development is influenced and shaped by both **genetic inheritance (nature)** and the **environment and children's life experiences (nurture)**. Some theories lean more towards nature as an explanation of development, and some lean more towards nurture.

For example, **Chomsky's** Language Acquisition Device (LAD) theory is based on the understanding that children are genetically pre-programmed (see page 22).

Nature: the influence of inherited features on development

The child

Nurture: the influence of the environment and experiences on development

For example, theories such as **Bandura's** social learning theory or **Urie Bronfenbrenner's** bio-ecological systems theory are based on the proposition that the environment influences development (see pages 30–31).

It is now widely accepted that both nature and nurture play a role in development.

Factors

Four key factors may influence children's growth and development.

 Biological factors
- Health conditions present at birth
- Long-term illness
- Genetic conditions
- Premature birth

 Environmental factors
- Housing conditions
- Diet and nutrition
- Quality of education
- Opportunities for play
- Access to resources

 Family
- Class
- Culture
- Quality of attachment
- Parenting style

 Life events
- Stress
- Accidents or injury
- Family breakdown
- Serious illness or death of main carer

Prenatal influences

A healthy lifestyle during pregnancy is critical. Poor lifestyle choices impact on the development of an unborn baby.

Poor lifestyle choices in pregnancy may result in low birth rate, and delayed brain and physical development that can continue to influence development later in life.

Unprescribed drugs

Alcohol

Stress

Infection

A poor diet

Smoking

Now try this

Suggest **two** possible positive effects and **two** possible negative effects of environmental factors on development.

11

Societal systems

Systems that impact on families' living conditions have an impact on children's development. Two key influences on physical development are **poverty** and **exclusion**.

Poor nutrition: contributing to poor health, delayed growth and physical development

Poor housing: leading to poor health and fewer opportunities for physical play

Poverty

Financial difficulties: causing stress and ill health; limiting education, play and leisure opportunities

Fewer play opportunities: leading to poor strength and stamina, and delayed gross motor development

Exclusion

Parents and children may feel excluded from society and services for a number of reasons. They may have:

- learning or language difficulties
- poor English language skills
- a disability/sensory difficulty
- mental health problems
- addiction to alcohol or drugs
- gender expectations, such as a belief that girls or boys should not take part in particular subjects or activities
- cultural/religious beliefs that are not shared with the local community
- financial difficulties, for example, being unable to meet the cost of childcare/leisure activities.

Impact of exclusion

- Being unable to access health services can lead to undiagnosed health or development problems that lead to delays.
- Being unable to feel part of the community will lead to poor self-image and low self-esteem, leading to stress.
- Children will have less opportunity to take part in physical activity, leading to delayed gross motor development.
- Children may not be able to attend a playgroup or nursery because of access or financial reasons, reducing opportunities for play.

Access to services

Families may be excluded from access to services because of **availability** or their **individual circumstances**.

- Service availability may differ in different areas.
- Childcare services may not be available locally.
- There may be restrictions on delivery or opening times of services, such as GP surgeries.
- There may be limited access to services for parents with other children to care for or parents working long hours.

- There may be limited availability or waiting times caused by pressures on services, such as children's mental health, physiotherapy.
- There may be learning, communication or sensory difficulties that impact on a parent/carer's understanding of, and contact with, available services.

Now try this

Meena is 4 years old. Her father has just lost his job so the family has moved to a poor housing area in a large city where they do not know their neighbours.

Give **two** examples of the effect of exclusion and poverty on Meena's physical development.

Physical activities

Physical development can be promoted through many different types of play and activity.

Physical exercise

Opportunities for exercise are essential for healthy growth and development. Activities may include:

- climbing
- ball games
- sit-on toys
- digging/planting.

The benefits of exercise for growth and physical development include:

- healthy heart and lung function
- stamina
- muscle tone
- balance and coordination.

Physical activities have benefits for growth and development

Indoor and outdoor activities

Provide opportunities for physical activity indoors and outdoors so that different aspects of physical development can be promoted.

- **Indoor play**, such as construction equipment, mark making and drawing or playdough – for the development of hand–eye coordination and fine motor control. Children can explore and use construction materials, modelling materials and cooking ingredients.
- **Outdoor play** such as climbing frames, gardening and ride-on toys – for the development of stamina, muscle development, balance and coordination. Children can explore and use natural materials such as logs, fir cones and sand, and tools for digging.

Baby and toddler

Activities to support physical development must be age and stage appropriate. Here are some ideas for supporting babies and toddlers.

Age	Activity	Physical development
Up to 6 months	✓ Coloured mobiles ✓ Rattles ✓ Play mat to encourage movement	✓ Stretching and reaching out ✓ Coordination ✓ Whole body movement
6 months to 12 months	✓ Activity rhymes, e.g. pat-a-cake ✓ Balls to encourage crawling ✓ Stacking and nesting toys	✓ Coordinating arm movements ✓ Strengthening arms and leg muscles ✓ Hand–eye coordination
12 months to 18 months	✓ Push along toys ✓ Finger painting ✓ Stacking bricks	✓ Encouraging walking to strengthen leg muscles ✓ Hand–eye coordination ✓ Fine motor control and hand–eye coordination
18 months to 2 years	✓ Action rhymes and songs ✓ Balls to throw and kick ✓ Malleable materials such as playdough	✓ Coordination and control ✓ Developing large muscles in arms and legs, balance and control ✓ Developing small muscles in the fingers and hands

Now try this

Alicja is 11 months old. She goes to nursery while her parents work. She tends to sit and play with toys that are close by. Although she can crawl, she is reluctant to move around and explore the nursery.

Suggest **two** suitable activities and the required resources that would support Alicja's physical development.

Promoting development

Children's development can be promoted through **planned activities** that include provision for different types of play and physical care routines.

Physical play

Physical activity can support other aspects of development such as **creativity** and **imagination**.

Role play

Role play can take place indoors or outdoors. Children use their gross motor control when they run, climb or build a den, and fine motor control when they use a till, set a table or dress up. In role play children take on any role they wish in their imaginary world. A range of materials and resources are manipulated and symbolised to support different storylines.

Dance and movement

Dance and movement are effective to encourage physical development and involve the whole body. Activities include:

- moving to music
- activity songs.

The benefits of dance and movement for growth and development include:

- healthy heart and lungs
- balance and coordination
- strengthening limbs and joints
- gaining control of limbs.

Arts and craft

Children should be provided with a range of materials to manipulate. Art activities that promote creativity and imagination may include:

- painting
- collage
- junk modelling
- use of malleable materials.

Arts and crafts activities can encourage children to use their manipulative skills and hand–eye coordination to bring their own ideas to life.

Self-care

Children's physical development can be promoted by supporting them to become independent in self-care.

Routines

Support and provision of routines that are appropriate to a child's age and stage include:

- **nutritious diet** for growth, healthy skin, teeth and bones
- sufficient **sleep and rest** for the cells of the body to repair themselves, for brain growth and function, and physical growth
- **exercise** for improving lung capacity and heart function, strengthening bones and joints, and coordination skills
- **physical care** routines for bathing and teeth cleaning for maintaining healthy development.

Independence

Children need to be aware and learn how to be in control of their own body and hygiene needs to keep themselves safe and secure. They can be supported by:

- using **activities** to develop fine motor skills needed for independence in washing, teeth cleaning and dressing
- encouraging and praising **independence**
- **songs** and **rhymes** about own body
- **topics** on 'myself'
- **cooking** activities to learn about nutrition.

Now try this

Design a play activity that can support the physical development of a group of four children aged 3 years.

Cognitive development

Cognitive development is about how children **organise ideas** and **make sense** of the world around them.

Problem solving – needed to work things out and make predictions about what might happen

Moral development – needed for reasoning and making choices, and how to act towards self and others

Types of cognitive development

Abstract thought and creative thinking – essential for thinking and discussing things that can't be observed

Language development – essential to organise and express thoughts

Memory – essential for storing and recalling information

Cognitive milestones

1 **Birth to 6 months old:** from birth babies can use all their senses to understand the world around them. By 3 months old they take an interest in toys.

3 **1 to 2 years old:** between 1 and 2 years children develop a sense of self and recognise their own name. They use all their senses to explore. Their memory is developing so they can seek hidden toys.

5 **3 to 5 years old:** by 3 years old children are asking questions, counting up to 10 and can recognise some colours. At 4 years old, they recognise and produce patterns, classify objects and can share objects.

Birth 1 2 3 4 5 6 7 8

2 **6 months old to 1 year old:** babies understand the meaning of some words, and they begin to understand cause and effect such as what happens when they shake a rattle.

4 **2 to 3 years old:** children become more inquisitive, they remember past experiences and enjoy talking about pictures in books.

6 **5 to 8 years old:** at 5 years old children are using simple calculations using numbers. By 7 years old they will think more deeply, reason, talk about abstract ideas and plan.

Now try this

Sami is 3 years old and has just started nursery. He is meeting the expected milestones in cognitive development. Sami loves to paint, play with sand and build towers with wooden blocks.

Give **three** examples of how Sami's cognitive development will help him to take part in his play activities.

Language and communication

The **development of speech** can be explained through distinct phases. It begins with the pre-linguistic stage, progressing to the linguistic stage when words and then sentences are used.

Stages of language acquisition

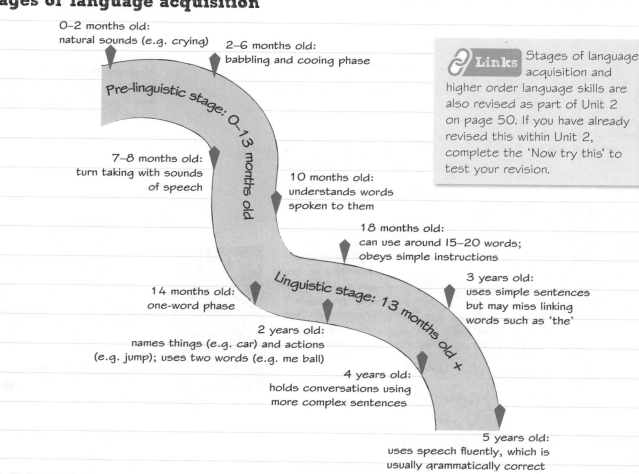

0–2 months old: natural sounds (e.g. crying)

2–6 months old: babbling and cooing phase

Pre-linguistic stage: 0–13 months old

7–8 months old: turn taking with sounds of speech

10 months old: understands words spoken to them

18 months old: can use around 15–20 words; obeys simple instructions

3 years old: uses simple sentences but may miss linking words such as 'the'

14 months old: one-word phase

Linguistic stage: 13 months old +

2 years old: names things (e.g. car) and actions (e.g. jump); uses two words (e.g. me ball)

4 years old: holds conversations using more complex sentences

5 years old: uses speech fluently, which is usually grammatically correct

Links Stages of language acquisition and higher order language skills are also revised as part of Unit 2 on page 50. If you have already revised this within Unit 2, complete the 'Now try this' to test your revision.

Higher order language skills

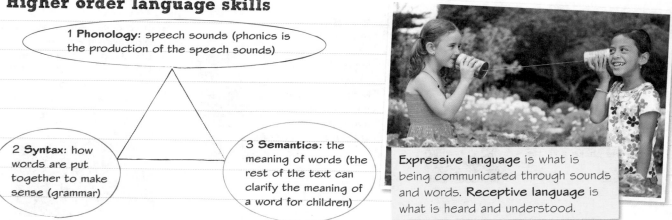

1 **Phonology**: speech sounds (phonics is the production of the speech sounds)

2 **Syntax**: how words are put together to make sense (grammar)

3 **Semantics**: the meaning of words (the rest of the text can clarify the meaning of a word for children)

Expressive language is what is being communicated through sounds and words. **Receptive language** is what is heard and understood.

Now try this

What is the approximate age of the following children? They are all meeting expected norms of language development.

(a) Micah cannot say 'teddy' yet but will give it to his dad when he says 'give me teddy'.

(b) Mia has just said to her friend 'Can I go on bike next?'

(c) Each time Bobby's mum says 'Hello' to him, he mouths and repeats 'oo' back to her.

Vygotsky

Lev Vygotsky believed social interaction with adults and other children was essential for **cognitive** and **language development**. For this reason his theory can be referred to as a **sociocultural approach**.

Cognition and language development

Vygotsky viewed children as apprentices in the learning process. The following four points help to explain how children learn according to Vygotsky.

1 Learning is an active process.

2 Cognitive and language development is the result of social interaction.

3 Children are apprentices who learn from others.

4 Language is important for cognitive development.

> 🔗 **Links** Vygotsky is also revised as part of Unit 2 on page 55. If you have already revised this within Unit 2, complete the 'Now try this' to test your revision.

Vygotsky's Zone of Proximal Development (ZPD)

Vygotsky believed that children could master skills with support and guidance from an adult or child who is more skilled. He called the level of skill the child could achieve alone the **Zone of Actual Development** (ZAD); what children could achieve with support he called the **Zone of Proximal Development** (ZPD).

The child's actual development	The child's potential development	
The Zone of Actual Development (ZAD)	**Zone of Proximal Development (ZPD)**	
What children know and can do independently	What children can achieve with support from an adult or child with higher level knowledge and skills	What children are unable to understand or do even with support

Increasing task difficulty →

Types of speech

Vygotsky differentiated between **social speech** and **private speech**.

☑ **Social speech** is used by children to communicate with others.

☑ **Private speech** is directed to the self and used for self-direction. It often accompanies children's play and helps to develop their thought processes.

Vygotsky believed that thought and language are separate systems until around the age of 3 years.

Supporting speech

In your practice this means:

- **using close observation** of children's current development to inform planning for their next steps (ZPD)
- using **questioning** and **modelling language** to develop language skills
- giving opportunities for **exploration** and **play** to develop private speech.

Now try this

Give **two** reasons why planned activities should take into account:

(a) what children already know and can do alone

(b) what they are likely to understand and be able to do with help.

Make reference to Vygotsky's constructivist learning theory.

Bruner

Jerome Bruner described the learning process as a 'spiral' where children can be helped to develop new ideas at a basic level which are then revisited and gradually become more complex.

Learning process

Bruner observed that:

- children need interaction to develop cognitive and language skills
- a language-rich environment with opportunities for social exchange is essential for children's cognitive and language development
- adults need to facilitate children's thought processes through a process called 'scaffolding'.

Scaffolding learning

Scaffolding describes the process of supporting children in their learning to help them reach the next level of cognitive and language development.

Examples of scaffolding in practice are:

- simplifying language
- motivating
- modelling language.

Bruner's modes

Bruner proposed three modes of cognitive representation.

1 **Enactive**: learning through physical actions. ⟷

Information gained through hands-on activity is stored in children's memory.

2 **Iconic**: image-based learning where children use one thing to represent another. ⟷

Pictures alongside words help children to store visual images.

3 **Symbolic**: understanding and using abstract symbols that represent ideas. ⟷

Children interpret symbols, including language, to form mental pictures.

Sustained shared thinking

Bruner and Vygotsky's theories help to explain **sustained shared thinking**, in which the adult works collaboratively with the child to extend their learning through sharing ideas and supporting problem solving.

Using extended conversations

Thinking aloud

Asking open-ended questions

Modelling thought processes

Speculating: 'I wonder what would happen if...'

Encouraging further thought

Clarifying ideas

Now try this

A group of 4-year-old children are planting cress seeds supported by an early years practitioner.

Give **two** examples of how they may use sustained shared thinking, referring to the theories of Vygotsky and Bruner.

Links To revise Vygotsky, see page 17.

Piaget: schematic development

Jean Piaget believed that children need hands-on experiences so that they can **construct** an understanding of the world around them. His theory is referred to as **constructivism**. His **schematic development theory** helps to explain how children think and learn.

Constructivism

Piaget's constructivist theory is based on the following four suppositions.

1 Children are active learners.

2 Children think differently from adults.

3 Children construct their own meanings from their experiences and the environment around them.

4 Language depends on the development of thought – cognition before language.

Schematic development

Children are active learners.

Assimilation: the child constructs an understanding or concept (schema).	The child has developed a schema about sand.
Equilibrium: the child's experience fits with their schema.	The child's experience in the nursery sand pit fits with their schema.
Disequilibrium: a new experience disturbs their schema.	Water is added to the sand pit. The sand acts differently so upsets the child's schema.
Accommodation: the child's understanding (schema) changes to take account of the new experience.	The child changes their schema to accommodate their new experience of sand. They go on to develop a new schema.

Differences in approaches

Here are three ways that Vygotsky and Bruner differ from Piaget. They believed instead that:

- the role of adults is more critical for facilitating language and cognitive development
- cognition is driven by language development rather than (as Piaget suggests) language by cognition
- with support children can progress more quickly than Piaget suggests in his stages.

Application

Here are ways that Piaget's constructivist theory can be applied to your practice.

- Activities should be provided that reflect children's stage of cognitive development.
- Opportunities should be planned for exploratory play to enable children to develop their thoughts and language.

Now try this

Define the word 'schema' that Piaget uses in his schematic development theory.

Piaget's stages

Piaget believed that children pass through four distinct **cognitive stages**.

Stages of learning

Age group	Stage	Learning
Birth to 2 years old	1 Sensorimotor	Babies learn about the environment and develop early schemas (concepts) by using all their senses to physically explore the world.
2 to 7 years old	2 Pre-operational	Children begin to control their environment by using symbolic behaviour including representational words and drawings and pretend play, but they are not yet able to think logically. They are **egocentric**, only seeing things from their own viewpoint.
7 to 11 years old	3 Concrete operations	Children use practical resources, such as counters for mathematics, to help them to understand. They classify, categorise and use logic to understand things they can see.
11 to 15 years old	4 Formal operations	Children have the ability for abstract thoughts. They can think rationally and solve problems.

Conservation

Piaget believed that children think differently from adults and, until the age of around 7 years, they are unable to reason and think logically, which he refers to as the ability to **conserve**. Piaget carried out research with children of different age groups to identify the stage when children begin to conserve.

1 This child is 4 years old. He is shown two identical glasses with the same amount of water.

2 The water from one glass is poured into a tall, narrow beaker.

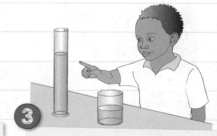

3 The child believes that the tall, narrow beaker has more water.

Piaget concluded from the test that:

- at the **pre-operational stage**, children cannot conserve because they cannot think about more than one aspect of a situation at one time
- by the **concrete operations stage**, children can think logically so they understand that the quantity of water stays the same when poured into a different shaped container.

Now try this

Nathan, who is 3, enjoys playing outdoors on the wheeled toys but gets frustrated when he has to wait his turn for a tricycle.

With reference to Piaget's theory:

(a) Why might Nathan find it difficult to wait for his turn?

(b) When will he start to see things from other children's perspectives?

Information processing

You need to know the concepts of **information processing** and **memory**. The brain uses a number of systems to process information from the environment. These are: **attention**, **perception** and **short-term memory**. Atkinson and Shiffrin's theory will help you to understand these concepts.

The process

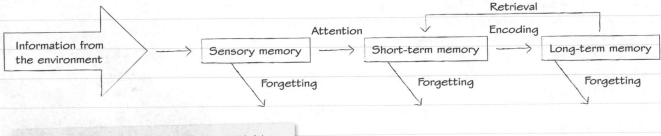

Atkinson and Shiffrin developed a model to show how the brain processes information.

Memory

Richard Atkinson and Richard Shiffrin proposed a **multi-store** model of memory. These memory types are related, but have different roles in information processing.

Memory type	Description	Links to cognitive development
Sensory memory	This is a **temporary** memory store. It works to screen information that is received from all the senses. The information is either transferred to the short-term memory or is forgotten.	**Babies** receive stimulus from the environment through their senses but are not yet processing information.
Short-term memory	This may be referred to as the **working memory**. It is used to construct meaning from the information and to respond to it. The number of pieces of information that can be held in the short-term memory is limited. Information may be transferred to the long-term memory or may be forgotten.	From the age of **2**, children are beginning to focus their attention and process information to form a response. They can recall some information from their past to apply to the present.
Long-term memory	This provides a large storage space for keeping information **long term** so that it can be recalled when needed. Some information from the long-term memory will be forgotten.	Children develop their long-term memory from around **3** years old. From the age of **5**, children can start to use information they have retained and apply it, such as their knowledge of phonemes as they read a book.

In practice

You can support children to develop attention and memory by:

* helping them to make **connections** between words/objects
* using **multi-sensory** activities
* giving **reminders**
* asking them to **sequence** events/stories
* supporting **language development** as it is critical to information processing.

Now try this

Ellie is 2½ years old. When she returned from a visit to the zoo with her father she went to her bedroom, set out her animals and pretended to feed them.

Give **two** ways that concepts of information processing help to explain Ellie's behaviour.

Chomsky and Skinner

Here are two opposing theories of language acquisition and development: **Chomsky** believed that children's brains are 'pre-wired' for language learning (**nature**) and **Skinner** believed that language learning must be reinforced (**nurture**) as a socially learned behaviour.

Chomsky

The **Language Acquisition Device (LAD)** was proposed by Noam Chomsky. It is the hypothetical part of the human mind that allows **babies** to acquire and produce language.

Chomsky suggested that humans:

- are born with a structure in their brain that enables them to acquire language
- have a critical period for initial language development during the first years of life
- all follow the same pattern of language development
- have an innate understanding of the structure of language (called **universal grammar**) that is the basis for all languages (subject, verb, object).

Chomsky's language acquisition theory helps to explain how children develop language skills. It is based on the nativist theory, which suggests that individuals are pre-programmed to develop in a certain way.

Skinner

BF Skinner proposed a **theory of reinforcement/repetition** to help to explain children's language development. He suggested that language is developed through:

- **reinforcement**: when babies use phonemes, they receive positive reinforcement from a carer so they repeat the sounds/words
- **repetition**: children learn by copying sounds and words they hear repeatedly.

Differences

Chomsky		Skinner
Because children have an innate ability to develop speech and language, it will happen naturally.	⟷	Children need stimulus to develop their speech and language.
Children are not influenced by 'adult' language use. Their pattern of development will be the same.	⟷	The language used around children will influence how they develop their language.
The adult role is not so important as, even if children are corrected, they will still develop their language in the same way.	⟷	The adult role is critical to support language through correction and reinforcement.

Now try this

Saira is 7 years old. She is meeting the expected stage in speech and language development.

Give **two** possible reasons that Saira is meeting her speech and language milestones with reference to:

(a) Chomsky's LAD theory

(b) Skinner's theory of language development.

Literacy

Literacy describes the development of reading and writing skills. **Cognitive development theories** help to explain how children develop their literacy skills and help practitioners plan for effective literacy support.

Recognising letters and words

Making marks and producing letter shapes

Linking sounds with written symbols

Reading and writing skills involve:

Understanding writing direction, e.g. in English, from left to right, top to bottom

Developing phonemic awareness

Understanding sentence structure

Applying theories

Theory	Description	Theory in practice
Schematic development theory (Piaget)	Children construct their knowledge about reading and writing by interacting with materials in the environment.	✓ Be aware of cognitive stages of development to provide age-/stage-appropriate activities. ✓ Provide opportunities and encourage children to explore a range of different writing and reading materials.
Zones of Actual and Proximal Development (Vygotsky)	Social interaction is important. Children need the support of adults or a more able child to progress from what they can already do to the next stage of literacy. Vygotsky called these the Zone of Actual Development (ZAD) and Zone of Proximal Development (ZPD).	✓ Identify the level of a child's skill and ability to be able to plan for the next stage. ✓ Support literacy activities using sensitive interaction and questioning.
Scaffolding (Bruner)	Children move through 'modes' or stages of development. They need social interaction to develop their literacy skills and progress by being **scaffolded** by an adult.	✓ Understand children's 'mode' of development to provide effective support. ✓ Provide support to help children to reach the next stage of development by scaffolding learning.
Information processing (e.g. Atkinson and Shiffrin)	Children construct understanding from their experiences using their short-term or 'working' memory. Some information is transferred to their long-term memory to be recalled at a later date.	✓ Read with children and get them to link pictures to words and to retell stories. ✓ Help children to make connections between the written word and spoken words.

🔗 **Links**   For more on Piaget's theory, revise page 19.
For more on ZAD/ZPD, revise page 17.
For more on Bruner's guided participation/scaffolding, revise page 18.
For more on information processing, revise page 21.

Now try this

Michael is 3 years old and has just started nursery. He appears to have had little experience of handling books and listening to stories. His key worker plans to develop his skills and interest in literacy.

Give examples of how schematic development theory and ZAD/ZPD might be applied to planning for support.

Communication

The development of language and communication is essential for children to interact with others and is closely linked with children's social development.

Verbal communication

Verbal communication involves the use of **sounds** and **speech** to **send messages**. Speech only forms a small part of children's communication. It is always accompanied by non-verbal forms of communication.

Non-verbal communication

Non-verbal communication is essential for **understanding**.

- **Eye contact** helps children to focus on what is being said.
- **Gestures** such as pointing, hand movements or nodding used alongside words and instructions aid understanding.

Forms of communication

Children with **additional needs** may be supported with **alternative communication** methods. Here are four methods.

 Makaton

Makaton is a **language system** that uses **signs** and **symbols** to help children with speech and/or language delay to communicate.

Children can learn to respond to the signs at an early age and then develop their use of signs. It can be used instead of, or to accompany, speech in order to aid understanding.

Makaton

 Sign language

British Sign Language is sometimes used with children who are deaf. Deaf children are often fitted with hearing aids or cochlear implants and can develop speech but they may choose to continue to use sign language to help with their communication.

British Sign Language

3 **Visual timetables**

Visual timetables can help children who have limited communication skills, English as an additional language or additional learning needs, to understand the routine of a setting. They are also helpful for children new to a setting.

 Activities
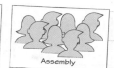 Assembly
 Circle time
 Choosing
 Creative development
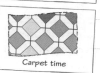 Carpet time

 Gestures

Gestures can be used alongside speech to support children to understand what is being said. For example:

- pointing to an object while saying a word
- nodding to indicate understanding
- facial expression to show positive emotion and interest
- gestures to support the meaning of individual words or instructions.

Now try this

Identify **two** examples of how you have used each of the types of non-verbal communication in your own practice.

Numeracy

Theories help to explain **stages of cognitive development** and help practitioners to promote children's **understanding** of numeracy, including logic, rules of number and recognising patterns.

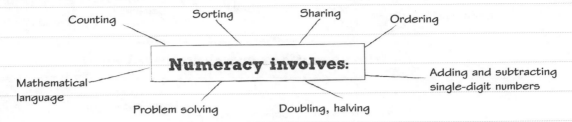

Counting   Sorting   Sharing   Ordering

Numeracy involves:

Mathematical language

Adding and subtracting single-digit numbers

Problem solving   Doubling, halving

Applying theories

Theorist	Theory	Theory in practice
Schematic development theory (Piaget)	Children construct their knowledge about number by **interacting** with their environment and by **exploring** mathematical materials.	✓ Point out numbers that appear in the environment. ✓ Provide opportunities for children to sort, order, match and count objects in their play.
Zone of Actual and Proximal Development (Vygotsky)	Children need the **support** of adults or a more able child to progress in numeracy skills from the Zone of Actual Development (ZAD) to the next stage, which Vygotsky called the Zone of Proximal Development (ZPD).	✓ Identify the level of a child's skill and ability to plan for appropriate activities. ✓ Support number activities using sensitive interaction and questioning, introducing numerical terminology.
Scaffolding (Bruner)	Learning is described as a **spiral** because children build on their previous learning. Children progress in their learning through being **scaffolded** by an adult.	✓ Understand children's stage of number development to support them towards the next level of understanding. Use sustained shared thinking to develop children's thinking and problem-solving skills.
Information processing (e.g. Atkinson and Skinner)	Children **construct** understanding from their number **experiences** using their short-term or 'working' **memory**. They transfer some information to their long-term memory to be recalled at a later date.	✓ Get children to share out objects and find the correct numeral to match to the group. ✓ Help children to make connections between the number of objects in a set and the written number.

🔗 **Links**   To revise schematic development theory, see page 19.
To revise ZAD/ZPD theory, see page 17.
To revise guided participation/scaffolding, see page 18.
To revise information processing, see page 21.

Now try this

Helena is 2½ years old. She is already noticing numbers in the environment. Her mother points them out and now she recognises and points out the number '3' on her door and the number '5' on the bus that she catches to nursery. She can count to five, although not always in the right order.

1 Suggest an activity that would help Helena's development in number skills.
2 Use the different theories you have learned about to explain Helena's numeracy development.

Mathematical concepts

An understanding of theories helps practitioners to plan for supporting children's mathematical concepts, language and problem-solving skills.

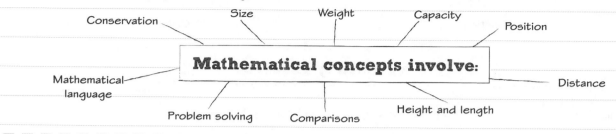

Conservation · Size · Weight · Capacity · Position

Mathematical concepts involve:

Mathematical language · Problem solving · Comparisons · Height and length · Distance

Development of concepts

The early years settings must provide opportunities for children to explore materials and resources for the development of **mathematical concepts** and **language**. The importance is explained by Piaget's theories of cognitive development.

Theories	Early years practice	Links to Piaget's theories
Schematic development	Provide resources that are changed frequently for hands-on experience to include: 2D and 3D shapes, sand and water play with different-shaped containers, playdough and balance scales.	**Children are active learners.** They need to interact with their environment and resources to develop ideas. As they play, they develop **schemas** which they build on when provided with new activities. 🔗 **Links** To revise Piaget's schematic development theory, see page 19.
Stages of cognitive development	Use assessment to understand the stage of development children have reached. Provide concrete materials or physical activity to help children to develop their understanding, such as handling 3D solids, and striding across a room to measure its length.	**Babies use their senses** to construct meaning about shape, space and measures up until the age of 2 (sensorimotor stage). From the age of 2, children use objects and symbols in their play to help them to construct ideas about mathematics. At the age of 7, they think logically about mathematical concepts. This means they can **conserve**. For example, they will understand that when a piece of dough changes shape, it will still weigh the same. 🔗 **Links** To revise Piaget's stages of development and conservation, see page 20.

Views

Unlike Piaget, Vygotsky and Bruner believed that children can be supported by an adult or more able child to progress to a higher stage of development. In practice, this means interacting with children as they play, asking open-ended questions, encouraging, praising and modelling. Bruner refers to this as **scaffolding**.

Scaffolding children involves a process of **sustained shared thinking**. Children need to be helped to make comparisons and construct hypotheses – 'Which holds more?', 'What would happen if...?' – and solve problems about shape, space and measures.

🔗 **Links** To revise more on Vygotsky and Bruner, see pages 17–18.

Now try this

Nathan, who is 3 years old, enjoys playing in the sand tray at nursery.

1   Suggest resources that could be put in with the sand to help Nathan's understanding of basic mathematical concepts such as those above.

2   Give examples of ways an adult could interact with Nathan with reference to two theories you have studied.

Exploring the environment

Children have a natural curiosity about their environment, which can be promoted and supported by best practice and by making links to different theories of learning. Some key theories and concepts are listed below.

Exploration

Children make sense of their environment by communicating their knowledge and observing:

- materials and their properties
- patterns
- similarities and differences
- people

- the natural world
- places
- how things work.

Activities

Here are some examples of activities children may engage in.

A 2 year old is playing with natural materials including hard materials such as shells, buckets and spades, and soft materials such as sand.

Staff provide resources for children to role play with.

A group of 6-year-old children are taken out to explore the woods. They collect leaves, sticks and wood and go on to build a den.

Theories

Here are ways that adults can support learning based on different theories.

Piaget viewed children as active learners. The adult is providing opportunities for the child to explore different materials. This is important for them to construct their own schemas (concepts) about materials (schematic development theory).

Bruner suggested adults could be play partners to scaffold the child's learning by giving new vocabulary such as 'hard' and 'soft' and helping them begin to understand similarities and differences in materials.

The concept of information processing. Visits in the wider community help children to process new information. Some information will be retained in their long-term memory, which they will recall and communicate verbally, in their play or through their drawings or writing.

Bronfenbrenner's bio-ecological systems theory builds links between the child, their immediate environment and the wider community, influencing children's holistic development.

Vygotsky's Zone of Proximal Development. Providing challenging experiences helps children to progress to the next level of thinking.

Sustained shared thinking. Using questioning to get children to develop their ideas to plan and use logic to build their den.

Now try this

A group of 4-year-old children are given technological toys that have gears and pulleys to explore.

Use schematic development theory and the concept of information processing to help to explain the purpose of providing this type of activity.

Emotional development

Emotional development is about how children develop their sense of self, their feelings towards themselves and others, and how they cope with their feelings.

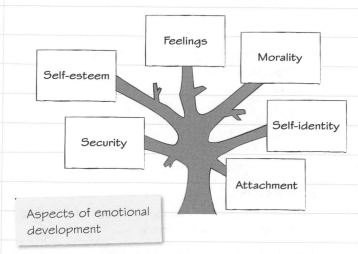

Aspects of emotional development

Young children find it difficult to control their feelings and need support from an adult.

Stages

Age group	Milestones of emotional development
Birth to 6 months	By 1 month old babies are already showing feelings through expressions. By 3 months old they will show pleasure when given attention.
6 months to 1 year	By 6 months old babies may show distress when their main carer leaves. By 9 months old they are beginning to display their likes and dislikes. They often need a comfort toy or blanket to help them to cope with their emotions.
1 to 2 years	By 12 months old moods tend to change quite quickly. Babies are still dependent on their comfort toy and like to have reassurance from an adult. By 18 months old they are easily frustrated. They alternate between being clingy and rejecting help.
2 to 3 years	By 2 years old children can express how they feel but often have tantrums when they are misunderstood. They are becoming more independent but can often be clingy. At $2\frac{1}{2}$ years old they may show signs of jealousy of other children.
3 to 5 years	By 3 years old children are developing a sense of morality, and they understand and follow rules. They start to have best friends and show affection to others. By 4 years old they show increasing sensitivity towards others. They understand right from wrong.
5 to 7 years	By 5 years old children show sympathy to others and begin to understand the concept of fairness. By 6 years old children are beginning to compare themselves to friends and developing their self-image. By 7 years old they are more able to control their feelings.

Impact

Emotional development has a wide-ranging impact on:

- **cognitive** development: an inability to cope with feelings may affect attention, memory and thought processes
- **social** development: self-image, both positive or negative, impacts on children's ability to relate to others
- **growth**: anxiety may impact on health, growth rate and physiological development.

Now try this

Jacob is 2 years old. Recently he has started snatching toys from other children. When they are given back to the other child he begins to scream and it takes some time for him to control his temper.

Describe **two** reasons why Jacob might display this behaviour at his life stage.

Social development

Social development is about how children develop skills and attributes that enable them to live within the family and community.

Independence   Confidence   Friendships

Social development involves:

Turn taking   Wider relationships

Sharing

Developing friendships

Children begin to develop friendships from around the age of 3.

- **Up to the age of 3** children are still reliant on attachments to their main carer or siblings.
- **From the age of 3** children can take turns, communicate easily and so enjoy playing with other children.
- **After the age of 4** children choose their own special friends. They learn to interact positively and cooperate.
- **From the age of 5** they often choose friends of the same sex. They enjoy spending time with their wider family and friendship groups.

The ability to develop friendships impacts on all the other areas of children's development.

Impact on growth and development

Social development has a wide-ranging impact on:

- **emotional** development: through social interactions children learn how to manage their own feelings and recognise the feelings of others
- **cognitive** development: through social play children explore new ideas and materials. They learn from other children who are more skilled (see Vygotsky's ZPD theory on page 17)
- **growth** and **physical** development: children with positive social development join in with games and physical activities that promote health and growth
- **speech and language**: through social interactions children learn new vocabulary and learn how to listen and express their ideas.

Now try this

Saeed is 4 years old and has just started school. He has a best friend called Nathan.

Give **two** examples of the possible effects of starting school on Saeed's social development.

Behaviour: Bandura and Skinner

Theories help to explain why children behave in particular ways. Understanding these can support early years practice.

Bandura's social learning theory

Albert Bandura's social learning theory is based on a belief that learning happens through **observing**, **imitating** and **modelling** the behaviours of others.

The four principles of social learning.

1 **Attention:** learning takes place when a child focuses their attention on a person who 'models' the behaviour. Children are more likely to imitate the actions of someone they identify with or admire.

2 **Retention:** what has been observed is retained in the child's memory to be used when an opportunity occurs.

3 **Reproduction:** what has been learned is reproduced/imitated. It may be rehearsed in the child's mind first and then imitated at a later stage when there is an opportunity.

4 **Motivation:** children feel motivated because they anticipate intrinsic or extrinsic rewards (vicarious reinforcement). Children will be motivated to repeat or cease the behaviour depending on intrinsic or extrinsic reinforcement.

Skinner's operant conditioning theory

Skinner's **operant conditioning theory** was based on his belief that learning could be shaped by controlling the environment.

- The environment influences behaviour through reinforcers.
- Positive or negative experiences that follow a behaviour influence a child's response.

In practice

👍 Positive reinforcers can be giving stars or stickers or praise.

👎 Negative reinforcers may be taking away a responsibility such as being a snack monitor or showing displeasure through facial expression.

Positive reinforcement

The behaviour is repeated because of a feeling of self-efficacy and empowerment or because of rewards.

Negative reinforcement

The behaviour is not repeated in order to avoid an adverse experience such as lack of satisfaction or avoiding an adverse reaction.

Remember: Reinforcement may be positive or negative.

Negative reinforcement is not the same as punishment.

Bandura's Bobo doll experiment

In Bandura's Bobo doll experiment, children were shown adults being aggressive or non-aggressive towards the Bobo doll. The aggressive adults were either rewarded, reprimanded or had no consequence for their behaviour. The experiment was designed by Bandura to show that children would copy the aggressive behaviour of another and that the outcome for the adult impacted on the likelihood of children copying the behaviour.

Children copied adults' apparent aggression and hit the doll.

Criticisms of Skinner

- Immediate rewards may not work to shape behaviour in the long term. Children need intrinsic motivation.
- Skinner's theory was based on experiments with animals so may not explain the complex behaviour of humans.

Criticisms of Bandura

- Children are influenced by adults known to them but Bandura's Bobo doll experiment showed adults who were not known to children.
- His experiment does not show long-term effects on children.

Now try this

Use an observation from your own experience to explain Bandura's principles of learning.

⬅ Have you observed a child observing and imitating an adult's actions, such as using a computer, a telephone or digging in the garden?

Bronfenbrenner

Bronfenbrenner's bio-ecological systems theory helps to explain how **interconnected systems** within the environment may impact on a child's learning and development. The impact may be **positive** or **negative**.

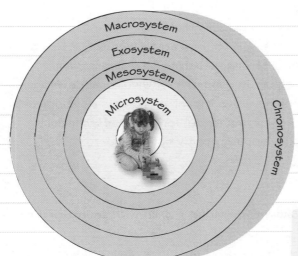

Bronfenbrenner's bio-ecological systems theory.

Systems

You need to understand five key systems and how they interact.

 Microsystem
Describes experiences and interactions within a child's immediate surroundings, their home, nursery or school and the people who are immediately influential such as a primary carer or key person.

 Mesosystem
Describes the interdependence of different parts of the microsystem and how they interact to influence a child's growth and development. For example, the impact that a positive (or negative) relationship between a parent and early years setting may have on development.

 Exosystem
Does not involve the child directly but does affect their growth and development. For example, the type of work a parent does, if a parent loses their job, or if a father often works away – these things may impact on the quality of the child's life and affect developmental outcomes.

 Macrosystem
This system involves the wider society outside the control of the family but still influencing their situation. This includes the economy and political, cultural or religious values. For example, the government introducing free childcare places or the availability and access to health services for families.

 Chronosystem
A chronosystem involves the timing of events and interacts with all other systems. For instance, in a child's personal life, events such as the age when they start nursery or age when parents split up may affect how well they cope. Chronosystems may involve events in the wider world such as war, which results in a child becoming a refugee.

Criticisms of Bronfenbrenner

- He did not pay enough consideration to the biological influences on development such as a child's resilience.
- He did not pay much attention to cognitive milestones linked to physiological change in explaining influences on development.

Now try this

Using an example from your own experience relating to microsystem and mesosystem stages from Bronfenbrenner's theory, explain how these two systems are interdependent.

Attachment: Bowlby and Ainsworth

Attachment is the **emotional bond** that is formed between babies and young children and their caregiver. Here are theories that help to explain the **attachment process**.

Bowlby

John Bowlby's **theory of attachment** suggests that:

- babies are biologically pre-programmed to form attachments
- in the early months babies form a strong attachment to the mother
- attachment to the primary caregiver is essential for emotional development
- a disruption to attachment has a negative impact on holistic development
- attachment to the primary caregiver is a model for future attachments
- infancy is a critical period for developing positive attachments.

Internal model

Bowlby believed that **early attachment** provided a child with an **internal model** that influenced all other attachments throughout their life.

- Positive attachments at an early stage provide security, which would lead to the development of positive relationships throughout life.

- Being rejected and unloved at an early stage would lead to difficulty in forming relationships in later life.

Ainsworth

Mary Ainsworth's **Strange Situation Classification (SSC)** classified attachments into four main types based on a study of children's reactions when parted from a parent.

	Secure	Insecure/avoidant	Insecure/resistant	Disorganised/disorientated
Parenting style	In tune with the child and their emotions	Unavailable to the child/rejects them	Inconsistent in meeting the child's needs	Ignores the child's needs; abusive behaviour
Child's behaviour	Will show distress when primary caregiver leaves and greets them on return. Happy with strangers when caregiver is present.	Does not show distress when primary caregiver leaves. Continues to explore the environment. May go to stranger for comfort.	Shows distress when primary caregiver leaves but resists contact on their return. Shows anxiety and insecurity.	Looks for security but is distrusting. Looks or moves away from primary caregiver.

Criticisms

- **Bowlby** believed that attachment is an instinctive survival mechanism and young babies form an attachment with one carer. In later research, theorists such as Rudolph Schaffer and Peggy Emerson also observed how in the first months babies could form attachments with more than one carer.

- **Ainsworth** has shown that, rather than the process being similar for all babies as Bowlby suggests, parenting may affect the quality of attachments.

Now try this

Ruby is 1 month old. Her mother has formed a strong bond with her. She recognises and understands her needs. She intends to return to work when Ruby is around 6 months old and Ruby will go to a nursery full time.

With reference to Ainsworth's classifications, outline how going to nursery may affect Ruby.

Family systems

Young children spend the majority of their time with their family. It is the primary unit that provides experiences and support that has a significant influence on growth and development.

Family influences

Positive   **Negative**

👍 **Strong family systems** provide stability and the conditions children need for promoting growth and development. A parent's positive educational experiences lead to positive support for their child's learning.

Family system, educational background of parents, social class, employment status.
(Links to Maslow's hierarchy of needs.)

👎 **Families that have low income and social class** may experience poor housing conditions and poor diet that impact on children's emotional development and learning. They may not grow as expected and may experience more illness.

👍 **Consistent care and strong attachments** lead to high self-esteem, which help to promote social development. Positive relationships prepare children for learning at nursery and school. Children often display positive moral values they learn at home.

Parenting style including attachment behaviours, level of family harmony, moral values. (Links to Bowlby's and Ainsworth's attachment theories.)

👎 **Inconsistency in parenting and poor-quality attachments** lead to insecurity and difficulties in coping with change. It can lead to a negative self-image and low self-esteem. Children may grow to lack moral values if they do not experience moral values in the home.

👍 **Wider family and society** can provide support and cultural identity important for building effective relationships. It provides security that promotes emotional development and positive attitudes to learning.

Wider family networks, social cohesion and cultural identity.
(Links to Bronfenbrenner's bio-ecological systems theory.)

👎 **Poor family networks and lack of cohesion** can compound the negative effects of poverty and inconsistencies in parenting. This can lead to further stress resulting in poor emotional development.

Now try this

Give **three** reasons why early recognition of family difficulties is important for promoting and supporting children's development.

Supporting relationships

An important role of the early years practitioner is to support children's social development. You need to know how theories can be applied to early years practice.

Positive relationships

Here are four ways that practitioners can support positive relationships.

 Cooperation and collaboration

- Introduce games and activities that require turn taking.
- Provide home or shop play to encourage communication and cooperation to act out roles.
- Organise joint projects such as planting a garden or creating an art activity.

 Rules and boundaries

- Get children to agree rules for their play so they are more likely to follow them.
- Show, as well as tell, children what is expected of them.
- Give reminders or use pictures, such as the number of children playing in the sand.

 Modelling behaviour

- Be playful with babies to develop a positive relationship.
- Play alongside children to model ways to interact with others, including turn taking and being fair.
- Help children to use manners and show consideration to others.
- Build effective partnerships with the child and their parents.

 Dealing with conflict

- Use circle time to explore concepts such as fairness.
- Allow children time to resolve their own conflicts (if safe to do so) before stepping in.
- Talk to children about ways they resolved a problem.
- Use stories to illustrate ways to resolve conflict.

Bandura

Bandura's social learning theory is based on **observations** of children showing that their behaviour is conditioned by what they see others doing. This theory helps to explain the importance of modelling behaviours that, in turn, help to build friendships and relationships. Children will copy ways to interact appropriately such as taking turns or resolving conflict, which will help them to make friends.

 To revise more on Bandura, see page 30.

Bronfenbrenner

Bronfenbrenner's model is based on the belief that everything in the environment has a direct, or indirect, influence on growth and development.

The **microsystem** is the child's immediate environment. Supporting friendships and relationships in the early years setting and their home is critical for their overall development.

The **mesosystem** describes the importance of the strong links between the child's immediate environments, for instance home and early years setting, for positive growth and development. This helps to explain the importance of the key person building relationships with the whole family.

 To revise more on Bronfenbrenner, see page 31.

Now try this

Suggest an activity you could use in circle time to help children to explore how to deal with conflict.

Stages of play

Play is important for the development of friendships and relationships with others.

Play
- All children play.
- Babies start to play from the first few months of life.
- Play is particularly important in early childhood for emotional and social development.

Play progression
All children pass through these stages but the age they do so may vary. Initially children play alone, then alongside other children and eventually they share and cooperate during play.

Birth to 2 years old: solo play
In **solo play** children play alone with toys such as rattles, shakers and balls. They may be aware that other babies are present but do not attempt to play with them.

This child is engrossed in his own play.

These children are playing next to each other but involved in their own play.

Stages of play in infancy and early childhood

These children are sharing, talking and playing together.

2 to 3 years old: parallel play
During **parallel play** children are aware of other children and they may copy each other but they are not interacting. They will enjoy sand and water play, building blocks and small-world toys.

3 years old and over: cooperative play
In **cooperative play** children share ideas and resources in the same activity. They enjoy domestic and imaginative play where they can interact with each other to agree roles to develop their play towards a shared goal.

Links to Bruner

Bruner's three modes of cognitive representation help to explain the stages of play.
- At the **enactive stage** children are learning through the physical actions they use in their play.
- At the **iconic stage** they use one thing to represent another in their play.
- At the **symbolic stage** they can use abstract symbols to represent ideas in their play.

Links to Piaget

Piaget's stages of learning help to explain the stages of play.
- At the **pre-operational stage** (2 to 7 years old) children take part in pretend play and use symbols – one thing to stand for another – such as a stick representing a spoon.
- Using **symbolic play** helps children to take part in cooperative play.

 Links To revise Bruner's three modes of cognitive representation, see page 18.

Links To revise Piaget's stages of learning, see page 20.

Now try this

Tim is 20 months old. Identify suitable toys and resources that could be provided to encourage parallel play alongside his brother who is 3 years old.

Understanding self

Difficulties in children's emotional development can have consequences for other areas of development. Theories are used in early years settings to support children's understanding of self and others.

Support

Here are ways that practitioners can support **emotional development**.

Understanding of self

- Use praise to help children feel positive about themselves.
- Acknowledge children's individuality, including their home language.
- Build self-esteem through provision of age-appropriate activities in which they can succeed.

Developing a sense of morality

- Help children to think about alternative actions.
- Model positive behaviour and point out positive behaviour in children.

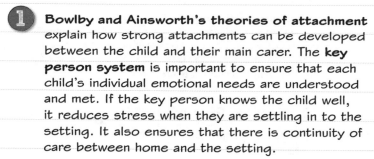

Dealing with emotions

- Give children individual attention to talk through how they feel.
- Give children words to help them to express their feelings.
- Use art activities or physical play to help to express feelings.

Understanding the needs of others

- Use stories to explore the feelings of characters that children identify with.
- Talk to pairs or small groups of children about how they feel following conflict.

Theories

These four theories help to explain early years practice.

1 **Bowlby and Ainsworth's theories of attachment** explain how strong attachments can be developed between the child and their main carer. The **key person system** is important to ensure that each child's individual emotional needs are understood and met. If the key person knows the child well, it reduces stress when they are settling in to the setting. It also ensures that there is continuity of care between home and the setting.

2 **Bronfenbrenner's bio-ecological systems theory** explains the importance of the interrelationship between home and the early setting. **Inviting parents or carers** into the setting and talking to parents about their children's needs and interests ensure that the child is understood and that there is continuity in care. The key person can work with the family to support their child's emotional development, such as their self-esteem and ability to deal with emotions.

3 **Piaget's stages of moral development** explain that from birth to 4 years old children learn right from wrong through their actions. From 4 years to 10 years, children believe that there are rules set by adults which are unchanging. Their actions are influenced by adult approval. By 7 years, children understand the concept of fairness and follow rules of play. Practitioners should model positive behaviour and show consistency in their responses. Children should be supported to agree rules for play.

4 **Bandura's social learning theory** explains how children learn by **watching** others. Modelling positive behaviour and showing sympathy and empathy with others will help children to develop a sense of morality.

Now try this

Give a further example of how early years practitioners can support each of the four theories relating to emotional development above.

Transitions

Everyone experiences transitions in their life that impact on their development. A transition such as starting school is expected and can be planned for. Transitions such as the break-up of the parents are unexpected.

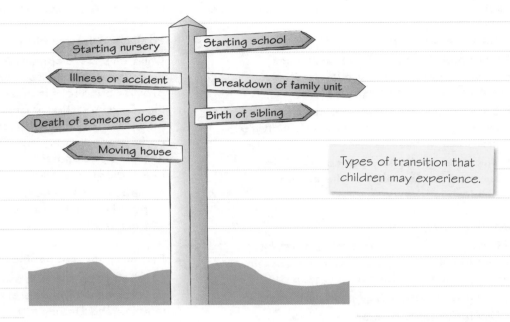

Starting nursery

Starting school

Illness or accident

Breakdown of family unit

Death of someone close

Birth of sibling

Moving house

Types of transition that children may experience.

Predictable transitions

These are life events that:

- are **likely** to happen to most children, such as starting nursery or school
- can be **anticipated** and **prepared** for.

Predictable events often have **positive effects**, particularly if children are starting new experiences they are looking forward to. They can help to build confidence and self-esteem. Transitions give opportunities to learn through new experiences and enable children to build new relationships. Although predictable events are expected, they can cause anxiety when routines change that may affect emotional development.

Unpredictable transitions

These are life events that:

- are **not expected**, such as **sudden** illness or injury of the child or their carer
- happen with **little or no warning** so **cannot be prepared** for.

Unpredictable events mean **changes** to a child's routines and sometimes mean separation from a main carer or from someone close to them.

Sudden changes can cause stress and anxiety which may impact on a child's sleep and eating patterns, affecting growth, concentration and the ability to learn. Unexpected transitions can affect a child's development in the short and long term. Negative effects can be minimised by helping children to prepare for transitions whenever possible.

Now try this

Anjana, who is 4 years old, is an only child. Her mother is expecting a baby in a few weeks' time.

1 Give **one** positive and **one** negative example of how Anjana's development may be affected by the arrival of the baby.
2 Suggest **two** ways to help Anjana to prepare for the transition.

Early years theories

Theories based on research of child development contribute to the development of early years practice.

Curriculum frameworks

Here are six aspects of an effective early years framework and how they are influenced by theories.

 Children are unique

Growth and development is influenced by **nature** (genetics) and **nurture** (the environment and experiences).

- **Early years practitioners** must be aware of, and take account of, children's individual needs.
- **The role of the key person** is critical for an understanding of the individual child.

 Enabling environments

Children are **active learners** so must be provided with a range of materials, resources and opportunities for play (Piaget).

- **Provide a range** of sensory materials.
- **Design interesting areas** indoors and outdoors that encourage children to explore.
- **Design areas for play** where children can choose and access their own resources.

 Balanced curriculum

Children need time to explore and construct their thoughts (Piaget). Social interaction with an adult or more able child can help to develop thought processes (Vygotsky and Bruner).

- **Provide a balance** of child-initiated and adult-led activities.
- **Give time** for children to explore materials and play imaginatively.
- **Use sensitive interaction** to support children to develop ideas and build on what they already know and can do.

 Positive relationships

Children's development is affected by insecure attachments. **Early attachments** provide a model for attachments in later life (Bowlby's theory of attachment). The **interrelationship** between parents and the early years setting impacts on children's holistic development (Bronfenbrenner's bio-ecological systems theory).

- **Appoint a key person** for developing positive relationships with the child and their family.

 Planning and assessment

Children pass through stages of development (Piaget's stages of learning and Bruner's three modes of representation). Children can be supported by an adult to progress to the next stage of learning by knowing (Vygotsky's Zone of Proximal Development).

- **Monitor** growth and development through observation and assessment.
- **Use assessment** for early recognition of atypical development.
- **Produce individual** support plans.

 Safety and security

For children to be able to reach their **full potential** they must have their **basic needs** met (Maslow's hierarchy of needs).

- **Assess risk** and develop policies and procedures to keep children safe and secure.
- **Plan routines** to include sleep, rest, a nutritious diet and exercise for growth and physical development.
- **Use observation** to identify children who may be at risk of harm or abuse.

Now try this

Working closely with parents can lead to positive outcomes for children's development. Give **two** reasons why this should be the case, using theories to support your answers.

Your Unit 1 exam

Your Unit 1 exam will be set by Pearson and could cover any of the essential content in the unit. You can revise the unit content in this Revision Guide. This skills section is designed to **revise skills** that might be needed in your exam. The section uses selected content and outcomes to provide examples of ways of applying your skills.

Exam checklist

Before your exam, make sure you:

✓ have a black pen you like and at least one spare

✓ have double-checked the time and date of your exam

✓ get a good night's sleep.

Check the Pearson website

The questions and sample response extracts in this section are provided to help you to revise content and skills. Ask your tutor or check the Pearson website for the most up-to-date **Sample Assessment Material** and **Mark Scheme** to get an indication of the structure of your actual paper and what this requires of you. The details of the actual exam may change so always make sure you are up to date.

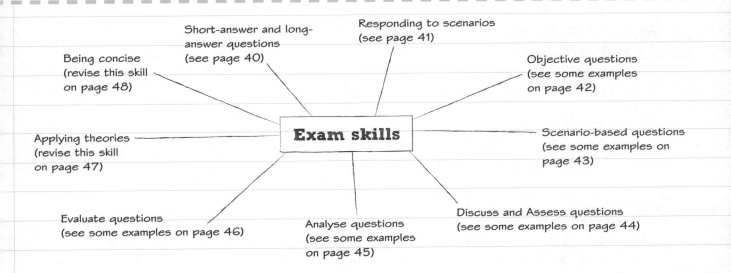

Being concise (revise this skill on page 48)

Short-answer and long-answer questions (see page 40)

Responding to scenarios (see page 41)

Objective questions (see some examples on page 42)

Applying theories (revise this skill on page 47)

Exam skills

Scenario-based questions (see some examples on page 43)

Evaluate questions (see some examples on page 46)

Analyse questions (see some examples on page 45)

Discuss and Assess questions (see some examples on page 44)

Now try this

Visit the Pearson website and find the page containing the course materials for BTEC National Children's Play, Learning and Development. Look at the latest Unit 1 Sample Assessment Material (SAM) to get an indication of:

- the number of papers you have to take
- whether a paper is in parts
- how much time is allowed and how many marks are allocated
- what types of questions appear on the paper.

Your tutor or instructor may already have provided you with a copy of the Sample Assessment Material. You can use this as a 'mock' exam to practise before taking your actual exam.

Short- and long-answer questions

Here are some examples of skills involved when answering short or long answer questions.

Answering the questions

All questions will assess your understanding of how the principles, theories and models of development apply to individual children.

When responding to short-answer questions, show your ability to:

- read each scenario carefully
- apply theory to the practical, real-life situations
- relate your answer to each scenario.

When responding to long-answer questions, show your ability to:

- analyse and interpret theories, how they relate to other domains of development and their impact on early years practice
- plan and write detailed answers.

 To revise long-answer questions, see pages 43–47.

Worked example

Carly is $3\frac{1}{2}$ years old. She goes to nursery each morning. Carly loves to join in with role play in the home corner or shop.

Describe two ways in which joining in with role play with other children will promote Carly's social skills.

 4 marks

 Here is an example of a short-answer question. Read the scenario carefully.

The question relates to the child described in the scenario so your answer should refer to Carly.

Sample response extract

1   When taking part in role play Carly will develop skills in negotiation to be able to take part in acting out roles and storylines in the play.

2   Carly will learn that she must cooperate with others so that she can share resources during the play.

 The question asks for 'two ways'. Give two numbered points to show that you have described two different aspects of social development.

 Look at page 43 for more on **Describe** questions.

Now try this

Identify **two** language milestones that Carly should have reached.

 To provide the correct response, you need to know the expected stage of language development.

 Look at page 16 to revise the content covered in this question.

Responding to scenarios

Scenarios may include one or more children in a family. They may include details such as **family background, age, skills and abilities, additional needs, environment** or **transitions**. Read each scenario carefully before answering any questions.

Applications

Scenarios enable you to apply your knowledge and understanding of the content of this unit to **realistic situations** and **contexts**. You may need to apply knowledge and understanding about:

- ✓ principles of growth and development
- ✓ patterns of physical, cognitive, emotional and social development from birth up to the age of 7 years 11 months
- ✓ factors that impact on children's growth and development
- ✓ theories that help to explain early years practice
- ✓ how early years practitioners can promote and support children's growth and development.

Worked example

Micah is 3 years old and meeting the expected milestones in physical development. He has just started nursery. The nursery has an outdoor play area with a climbing frame and ride-on toys.

Explain two aspects of Micah's gross motor skills at his age in relation to his ability to take part in outdoor play at nursery. **4 marks**

Sample response extract

1 Micah will have developed the large muscles in his arms and legs which will help him to hold on to the climbing frame and push up with his legs to climb higher.

2 Micah will be developing his balance and coordination so will be able to pedal and control ride-on toys.

 You could underline key words to help you to answer the question. In this example scenario, you could underline Micah's **age**, whether he is meeting his **expected milestones** and the types of **activities** he will take part in.

 You should **recall your knowledge** of the gross motor physical skills a child will have acquired by the age of 3, **making links** to how Micah will use them to take part in the activities.

 You should make sure that you **refer to Micah** and what he takes part in at nursery **specifically**, so that you do **not** give an answer about the general development of 3-year-olds.

🔗 **Links** To revise the content covered in this question see page 9, and for more about **Explain** questions see page 43.

Now try this

Identify the type of grasp that Micah would be expected to use when he draws a picture

- ☐ **A** simple tripod grasp
- ☐ **B** dynamic tripod grasp
- ☐ **C** pincer grasp
- ☐ **D** palmar grasp

 You may be asked to choose the correct answer from a choice of four.

 🔗 **Links** To revise the content of this question, see page 8.

Objective questions

Here are some examples of skills involved if answering objective questions.

Objective questions

You may be asked questions that use the **command** words: 'which', 'identify', 'give', 'list'.

- **Which**: you may need to select the correct item or feature from a definite set.
- **Identify**: you may need to indicate the main feature, purpose or qualities of something.
- **List**: you may need to give an item-by-item record.
- **Give**: you may need to give brief examples or a justification (reason) for something.

Features and facts

If answering objective questions, you must **recall** the **main features** or **facts** relating to children's development.

If you are unsure, do not spend too much time on your answer. Give the best answer you can and move on to a new question.

Worked example

> Aarif is 3 years old and his sister Sadia is just 6 weeks old. Aarif goes to nursery. He enjoys sorting his cars into sets of different colours. He can say how many he has in a set up to five. Sadia is due for her 6-week developmental assessment.

(a) Which area of development is Aarif demonstrating?

`1 mark`

Make sure you read the scenario carefully. In this example scenario, you are given information about two children at different ages and stages.

Sample response extract

☐ social   ☐ physical
☐ emotional   ☒ cognitive

You need to recall the **areas of development** and draw a cross in the box against the **one** correct answer. If you make a mistake put a clear line through it like this and draw the cross in the correct box.

(b) List three measurements that the health visitor will take to check Sadia's growth during her assessment. `3 marks`

Only the types of measurement are needed in this answer. You do not need to give details of how these are taken or recorded.

Sample response extract

1 Weight
2 Head circumference
3 Length

 Links To revise the content needed for this question, see page 1.

(c) Identify two physical milestones that Aarif will be expected to achieve at his age. `2 marks`

Read the question carefully. If you are asked for two milestones, don't give a greater number than asked for, so that you use your time wisely.

Sample response extract

1 Aarif will be able to run forwards and backwards.
2 Aarif will be able to balance when walking along a line.

Now try this

Give **two** reasons why starting nursery will promote Aarif's emotional development.

'Give' questions might ask for a set number of reasons, as in this question, or a set number of examples.

Scenario-based questions

Here are some examples of skills involved when answering scenario-based questions. You may need to show your understanding of principles, patterns, theories or models of development and apply them to the context of a scenario. You might be asked to 'describe' or 'explain' (below) or to 'discuss' (see page 44).

> Describe two ways that the information processing theory helps to explain Tommy's development.
>
> 4 marks

If answering a 'describe' question, give a **clear account** that shows **knowledge** of the facts and **main features** of the topic.

> Explain two factors that may have impacted on Sam's physical development.   4 marks

If answering an 'explain' question, demonstrate that you can **apply** your understanding of the subject and context of the question by **giving reasons to support** your opinions, views or argument.

Worked example

> Maisie, aged 3 years, and her brother Jamie, 12 months, attend Teddies Nursery. The staff provide plenty of opportunity for children to develop their play.
>
> Describe two ways that Piaget's stages of cognitive development can help practitioners to support Maisie and Jamie's play.   4 marks

When reading a scenario, notice the key points. This example scenario includes the ages and stages of two children, a nursery context, and a focus development of play.

Read the questions carefully. This asks for Piaget's stages of development so you need to **recall** the **two stages** that relate to Maisie and Jamie's age.

Sample response extract

1. Up to the age of 2 years, children are in the sensorimotor stage. This means that Jamie will learn best through using all his senses so should be given lots of opportunity to explore different resources and materials in self-directed play.

Don't simply describe each stage. You need to **show** that you **understand** the stages by **relating** them to play provision in the nursery appropriate for each child, as shown in these answers.

2. According to Piaget, from the age of 2 years until the age of 7 children progress to the ~~sensorimotor stage~~ pre-operational stage. Maisie should be given resources and props in her play that she can use to symbolise real life objects and events.

If you make a mistake, show it clearly by striking through it and writing in the correct words.

 Links   To revise the content covered in this question, see page 20.

Now try this

Now try an **explain** question.

> Helena is 2½ years old. She has advanced language skills for her age. She can name everyday objects and actions and is using simple sentences.
>
> Explain **two** ways in which Helena's language skills will support her emotional development.

You need to give two separate ways and provide valid reasons for each.

 Links   To revise the content for this question, see page 4.

Discuss and Assess questions

Here are some examples of skills involved if answering 'discuss' and 'assess' questions.

Show your skills

Consider how your response to 'discuss' questions might explore all the different aspects of the topic, considering how the different factors interrelate and their importance in their influence on the developing child.

In response to 'assess' questions, consider all the factors or events in relation to the child or children described in the scenario and decide which are most important or relevant to reach a conclusion.

Discuss and assess questions may require different levels of detail in the answer. The example response below is of a more detailed answer.

Plan

It is helpful to produce a brief **plan** for discuss and assess questions. Here is a brief plan for an assess question that could be asked in relation to the scenario given in the worked example below.

Assess the extent to which Mia's atypical development may affect other areas of her development.

1 speech and language vital for developing thought processes

2 speech and language helps to build friendships

Areas of development to consider:

4 conclusion: language critical or will result in short- and long-term developmental delay

3 behaviour problems/ frustrations if unable to express self

Worked example

In this example scenario, Mia is showing atypical development. A response would be **well balanced** by discussing **different reasons** for the importance of early recognition.

Mia is almost 4 years old. She has just started nursery. Assessment of Mia's development has shown that, although she is meeting expected milestones in other areas of her development, she has delayed speech and language skills.

Discuss the importance of early recognition of Mia's atypical development.

Sample response extract

Early recognition of language delay means that individual support can be put into place. Understanding Mia's specific language needs will help practitioners to plan for appropriate methods of communication such as the use of Makaton or pictures. Practitioners should work together and with Mia's parents to provide additional support such as reading stories and modelling language. Early recognition is also important for referrals to specialist support. The earlier that support is put into place, the more likely it is to be effective.

Language influences all other areas of development so it is important that delay is recognised so the impact is minimised. For instance on social and emotional development if Mia finds difficulty in interacting with other children and adults. If she cannot express her feelings in words she may show her frustration through unwanted behaviour.

This extract from a response **explores different reasons** for the importance of early recognition including understanding of individual needs so the most appropriate support and communication methods can be used. It also discusses working with parents and specialists to minimise the impact on other areas of development.

Mia and her language needs are referred to throughout the answer. It is important to show good **understanding** of the subject and **link** it to the context of the question, in this way.

 Links Look at page 24 to revise the content covered in this question.

Now try this

Add two more sentences about the importance of early recognition of speech and language delay for cognitive development.

Think about how language is needed to enable children to explore and develop ideas.

Analyse questions

Here are some examples of skills involved if answering an 'analyse' question.

Analyse

Being asked to analyse means breaking down the theme, topic or situation to explore the interrelationship of different aspects. Producing a brief plan before starting to write is useful for noting the key information.

Answering the question

Consider how your response to long-answer questions might:

 demonstrate accurate and thorough knowledge

apply knowledge to the context of the question

structure and balance your answer by showing competing viewpoints

use specialist language consistently and fluently

provide a **supported conclusion**.

Worked example

Analyse the role of the practitioner in early years settings in supporting children's cognitive development, with reference to cognitive theories of development.   12 marks

Sample response extract

Early years practitioners have a responsibility to recognise and meet the needs of individual children in the setting.

Piaget's stages of cognitive development help practitioners to understand how children think and learn at each age/stage of development which is important for assessment and curriculum planning. Piaget's cognitive learning theory explains the importance of practitioners providing a range of resources, materials and experiences for children to explore because children construct their understanding through all their senses when they participate in hands-on play activities. Although Piaget remains influential in the delivery of the early years curriculum, he did not stress the importance of interaction between practitioners and children.

The early years curriculum is also influenced by Vygotsky and Bruner's social constructivist theories which emphasise the importance of adult-led activity to balance child-initiated play.

The question asks you to refer to theories so the answer needs to include at least two relevant theories.

This extract from a response refers to different aspects of the practitioner's role including:
• assessment and planning
• the importance of exploratory play
• resource provision
• interaction to support learning.

You should link each aspect of the role to the relevant theory.

You should show that you understand the difference between Piaget's constructivist theory and Vygotsky and Bruner's social constructivist models. Positive aspects of different theories should be taken into account.

Now try this

Continue the sample response extract with some further sentences including:

(a) the role of the adult to support children's learning with links to Vygotsky and Bruner's theories of cognition

(b) a conclusion on the importance of theories in understanding the role of the adult.

Show links between Vygotsky and Bruner's theories of cognition and the practitioner's role to support sustained shared thinking.

 To revise the content for this question, see pages 17–18.

Evaluate questions

Here are some examples of skills involved if answering 'evaluate' questions.

Worked example

Evaluate how Bandura's social learning theory helps in understanding the behaviour of children in an early years' setting.

14 marks

Sample response extract

Bandura based his theory on observations of children in his Bobo doll experiment. He concluded that children learned behaviours by copying the behaviour of adults. He proposed four stages of development.

At stage one children observe the behaviour. This means that the adult should show positive behaviours because at stage two children will retain an image of what they have seen in order to reproduce it at a time when an opportunity occurs (stage three). Behaviours can be positive, such as sharing a toy, or negative, such as snatching a toy. Bandura's stage four explains why children are motivated to copy the behaviour they have observed. Children may see that adults get satisfaction from or reward for their behaviour so will copy them. If behaving in a certain way makes the child feel good and empowered they are likely to repeat the behaviour. Bandura refers to this type of positive reinforcement as intrinsic. Positive reinforcement may also be extrinsic. If children are given a sticker, for example, or an adult praises them they may repeat the behaviour so that they get another reward. Critics argue that extrinsic reinforcement is unlikely to be successful in the long term and that children need to be intrinsically motivated for long-term positive effects on behaviour.

Bandura also recognised the importance of negative reinforcement to deter children from repeating unwanted behaviours. He believed that children would not repeat behaviours if they did not get satisfaction from it. They would also be keen to avoid negative effects such as not being chosen to play with other children.

Critics of Bandura suggest that he does not take into account the influence of the child's predisposition or nature in influencing behaviour and that genetic inheritance can influence a child's temperament.

On balance, Bandura's social learning theory is helpful in explaining how children develop their behaviour and it shows the importance of practitioners displaying consistent positive behaviour. Even though young children may have a natural predisposition to behave in a certain way, they can often be observed copying behaviours of others.

Answering the question

Evaluate questions may require extended answers that consider:

- ✓ strengths and weaknesses
- ✓ advantages and disadvantages
- ✓ relevance or significance, e.g. of a theory, factor or life event.

This extract from a response refers to investigations carried out by theorists, such as Bandura's Bobo doll experiment, and how they help you to understand the theories. Unless you are specifically asked to explain theories, you should only refer to the conclusions that are drawn from them in your answers.

You should give examples to support your understanding of the theory.

The extract correctly refers to negative reinforcement and does not confuse it with punishment.

You should consider alternative views in your answer. This will help you to reach a good conclusion.

You should refer back to the question in your conclusion so the links are clear.

 Links To revise more on ways to apply theory, see page 47, and for more on the content covered in this question, see page 30.

Now try this

Read through the sample response extract again. Note down where the learner has shown:

(a) the significance of Bandura's theory in explaining development

(b) strengths and weaknesses of Bandura's social learning theory in relation to development.

Applying theories

Theories help to explain children's development and early years practice. Here are some examples of skills involved when showing your understanding of theories in relation to the context of scenarios and the questions you may be asked.

Making links

Make sure that you show that you can **understand and explain** theories, and also that you can **make links and apply** the theories to the context of the question. Both aspects are important in your answer.

Selecting relevant theories

The specific names of the theorists or theories may not always be given in the question. Show that you can select relevant theories that support your views.

Worked example

Liam is $2\frac{1}{2}$ years old and he will be starting nursery soon. He loves to share books with his mum and talks about the pictures. He already knows and uses over 200 words. Liam is starting to link words together using object and verbs such as 'me drink it'.

Assess how theories of language acquisition help to explain Liam's language development.   8 marks

Make sure you read the scenario carefully. In this example scenario, information is given about Liam's age and stage of development.

Sample response extract

In their first few years children are at the critical period for language acquisition. Liam is making the expected progress for his age.

According to Chomsky's Language Acquisition Device (LAD) Liam has an innate ability to learn language and will be able to structure language using nouns and verbs in the correct order at his age. Chomsky referred to this as universal grammar that all children acquire whichever language they speak. This explains why Liam can already structure simple sentences.

Chomsky felt that language acquisition is influenced by nature and that adults have little influence on the process. This could explain why Liam may still make errors in tenses or miss out words even though he hears his mother using language correctly.

Critics of Chomsky suggest that he did not take account of the influence of adults and how children's language may be 'nurtured'. Liam's language skills are likely to have been helped by his mother, who shares books with him.

Skinner's operant conditioning theory explains how children's language can be reinforced by interaction so Liam is likely to imitate his mother's speech.

 This extract from a response shows the expected milestones for Liam at his age and takes account of this when exploring language acquisition theories.

 You should explore Chomsky's influential **Language Acquisition Device** (LAD), which is important to include when answering questions about language development.

You should give **a balanced answer** by including **critics** of Chomsky's LAD and Skinner's operant conditioning theory and explaining how it is likely that nurture as well as nature influences language development.

🔗 **Links** For more questions that require you to apply theories, see pages 43, 45 and 46.

Now try this

Write **three** more sentences to continue the sample response extract. Come to a balanced conclusion about the influence of Chomsky's LAD and Skinner's operant conditioning theory.

 Come to a conclusion about the influence of nature and nurture in language development.

 🔗 **Links** To revise the content needed for this question, see pages 22 and 30.

Being concise

Being concise means answering questions without adding unnecessary information.

Relevant answers

In long-answer questions a brief plan of key ideas/words will help you to keep to the point. Being concise is important because:

✓ the time you have available to answer each question is limited

✓ you will not gain extra marks by adding information that is not relevant.

Worked example

> Ellie and Thomas Carter have two children: Sadie, aged 3 years and Marc, aged 6 years. They live in a 10th-floor tower block where lifts are often broken. They are on the re-housing list as the flat is small and cramped and the bedrooms are damp. Ellie does not like to take the children to the local playground as there has been a lot of anti-social behaviour.

Explain two ways in which the family's housing situation may impact on Sadie and Marc's development.

4 marks

In this example scenario there is key information about a housing situation that could affect children's development, that should be referred to in a concise way.

Sample response extract

1   The family's housing is poor quality because it is on the 10th floor, cramped and damp. This is likely to cause stress for the whole family. Sadie and Marc will be aware of their parent's stress and will also be affected. This can impact on their emotional development because they will have poor self-concept. Having a poor self-concept is likely to result in poor self-image.

2   Sadie and Marc may not be taken to the park by Ellie because when the lifts are not working it is a long way down from the 10th floor. She will also be worried about the anti-social behaviour in the area. This means that the children will not have the opportunity to go on apparatus such as swings and climbing frames. This type of exercise is important to help them to develop their gross motor skills, coordination and balance.

An explanation will **not be concise** if you have repeated information from the scenario. Although the scenario should be referred to, you do not need to include the detail in your answer.

An explanation will **not be concise** if you add some unnecessary information such as the 10th floor.

Improved response extract

1   The cramped conditions and damp will cause Ellie and Tom to feel stressed, impacting on Sadie and Marc. This may negatively affect the children's self-concept resulting in low self-esteem.

The learner has produced a **concise** explanation. They have **included key information** and omitted any unnecessary words and information.

Both answers give valid examples of the possible impact on the children's development and would be given marks, but it will have taken more time to write the answer that is not concise. This means that time is lost that could be used for other questions.

Now try this

Rewrite explanation 2 from the sample response extract in two concise sentences, ensuring that you include the key information.

With reference to the scenario, suggest what impact the family's circumstances might have on the children's physical development. Give reasons for your answer.

Communication

Communication is the means by which information is sent and received. Lots of communication happens without speech and is described as '**non-verbal**'.

Non-verbal ways to support verbal communication

Here are four types of non-verbal communication that can aid children's understanding of verbal communication.

 Eye contact

Making eye contact with children helps them to focus on the meaning of what is being said. It helps to prevent other distractions.

In practice, making **eye contact** means:

- **getting down** to the child's level
- **waiting** until there is eye contact before speaking.

 Gesture

Used alongside words and instructions, gesture helps children to understand what is being said.

In practice, using **gesture** means:

- **pointing** to an object while saying a word
- **nodding** to indicate understanding
- **using facial expression** to show positive emotion and interest
- **using gestures** to support the meaning of individual words or instructions.

 Body language

Children pick up on the body language of adults. To prevent confusion, body language should match what you are saying.

In practice, using **body language** means:

- **having a relaxed** and open body position to show that you are receptive – for example, not crossing arms and legs
- **smiling** to encourage communication.

 Active listening

Active listening demonstrates interest in, and an understanding of, what someone is saying.

In practice, **active listening** means:

- **restating** – to show interest and active listening
- **clarifying** – asking further questions to show interest and check meaning
- **encouraging** – showing interest to promote confidence in speaking
- **paraphrasing** – expressing statements in different words to show interest and understanding.

Now try this

Identify examples of how you have used each of the four types of non-verbal communication in your own practice: eye contact, gesture, body language and active listening. Give **two** examples for each type of non-verbal communication, eight examples in all.

Language acquisition

The development of language happens in distinct phases. It begins with the **pre-linguistic** stage and progresses to the **linguistic stage**, when words and then sentences are used.

Stages of language acquisition

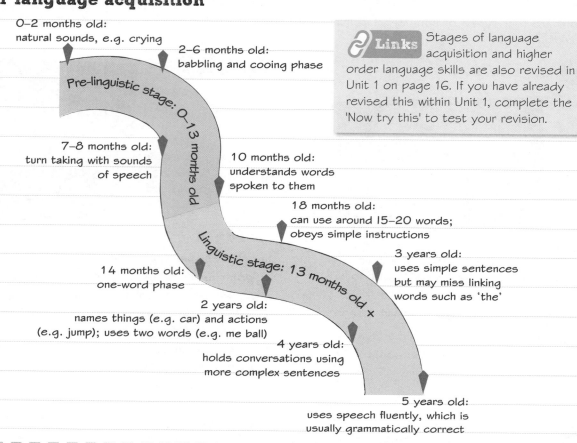

0–2 months old:
natural sounds, e.g. crying

2–6 months old:
babbling and cooing phase

Pre-linguistic stage: 0–13 months old

7–8 months old:
turn taking with sounds of speech

10 months old:
understands words spoken to them

18 months old:
can use around 15–20 words; obeys simple instructions

3 years old:
uses simple sentences but may miss linking words such as 'the'

14 months old:
one-word phase

Linguistic stage: 13 months old +

2 years old:
names things (e.g. car) and actions (e.g. jump); uses two words (e.g. me ball)

4 years old:
holds conversations using more complex sentences

5 years old:
uses speech fluently, which is usually grammatically correct

> **Links** Stages of language acquisition and higher order language skills are also revised in Unit 1 on page 16. If you have already revised this within Unit 1, complete the 'Now try this' to test your revision.

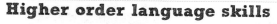

Higher order language skills

1 **Phonology** – speech sounds (phonics is the production of the speech sounds)

2 **Syntax** – how words are put together to make sense (grammar)

3 **Semantics** – the meaning of words (the context of a word in speech can help clarify the meaning of a word for children)

Language

Expressive language is what is being communicated through sounds and words. **Receptive language** is what is heard and understood.

Now try this

Ellie is 11 months old. She cannot make herself understood using words, so uses gestures to indicate how she feels and what she wants. For example, when she is happy she claps her hands.

Suggest other gestures that Ellie may use at her age.

Linked development

The development of **speech, communication and language** is closely linked with children's **social and emotional development**.

Behaviour – children who can express their feelings through speech and language are more able to control their emotions. Children with language delay may also experience behavioural problems.

Socialising – the ability to communicate verbally and non-verbally is essential for social play.

Speech, communication and language, and links to social and emotional development

Independence – well-developed speech and language gives children more control through the ability to make and express choices.

Self-esteem – the ability to express one's own ideas in play and activities leads to self-confidence.

Operant conditioning

Skinner's theory of operant conditioning is based on the belief that behaviour can be shaped by **reinforcement**.

Children learn language by being exposed to it.

↓

Children are rewarded for using language, so they repeat it.

Critics of Skinner point out that the theory does not explain why children do not model their speech on that used by adults around them, but develop their own 'rules' of speech'.

Learning from mistakes

Children's 'mistakes' in grammar form part of their language development.

- Overcorrecting can deter children from developing their speech.
- Repeating the sentence back in the correct form supports development.

Skinner suggested that parents responded to sounds and words that they recognised and ignored those they did not recognise.

Now try this

1 Give **three** examples of play activities that encourage the use of speech and language.

2 Suggest **two** ways in which adults can support children who have less well-developed speech in their play. Refer to Skinner's theory of operant conditioning.

In your set task you need to provide examples of play activities, and **explain** why they are appropriate with reference to relevant theories.

For question 2 you could suggest that adults repeat words that children have used. Make sure you explain why this will support speech development with reference to Skinner's theory.

Cognitive development

The development of speech, communication and language is closely linked with children's **cognitive development**.

Links

The meaning of words
Cognitive abilities that include an understanding of rules and principles of sentence structure (syntax), and developing their vocabulary to be able to develop abstract ideas

Links between speech, communication and language, and cognition

Information processing
Mental processes that help children to store, interpret and retrieve memories

Links between spoken sounds and written symbols
Remembering the shapes of sounds and symbols, making links to individual speech sounds and pronouncing them

Talking to children about their play and experiences to develop their ideas

Developing children's understanding of words and abstract concepts, so they can use them in speech

In your practice, helping children's cognitive development means:

Showing children how to recognise symbols in written form, to develop their reading and writing skills

Now try this

Mia and Ruby enjoy playing together in the domestic corner. Give **three** ways in which this opportunity for using language can support their cognitive development.

Chomksy and Brown

Chomsky believed that language is an innate skill that unfolds over time. **Roger Brown** was influenced by Chomsky. He developed a formula to explain stages of language acquisition.

Chomsky's Language Acquisition Device (LAD)

The LAD was proposed by **Noam Chomsky**. It is the hypothetical part of the human mind that allows infants to **acquire and produce language**. Here are four key features of Chomsky's theory.

1 Children are born with a structure in their brains that enables them to acquire language.

2 There is a critical period for language development in the first years of life.

3 Language development is part of the maturation process and follows the same pattern, becoming more complex.

4 Children have an innate understanding of the structure of language (called **universal grammar**) that is the basis for all languages (subject, verb, object).

Roger Brown's five stages of language development

Brown carried out a study of the speech of three children over time. He used a formula based on the **mean length of utterances** (MLU) and **morphemes** (units of grammar). He noticed that, in the early stages, children did make errors, such as in tense, but their word order (**grammar**) was correct. The length of sentences and inclusion of morphemes increased with age. Brown's **five stages** provide a useful **framework** for professionals to determine the stage of a child's language development and to predict the next stage.

Stage	Age	Example of language in practice
1	15–30 months	Joining two words, referred to as **telegraphic speech** (e.g. 'teddy gone')
2	28–36 months	Naming of objects, describing experiences with use of 'ing' endings (e.g. 'coming'), the inclusion of 'in' and 'on', and use of 's' plurals (e.g. 'cars')
3	36–42 months	Using past tense (e.g. 'went'), and possessives (e.g. 'Mummy's car')
4	40–46 months	Speaking sentences with more complex use of past tense (e.g. 'jumped') and articles (e.g. 'a', 'the')
5	42–52+ months	Making more complex sentences with use of contractions (e.g. 'we've') and third person irregular (e.g. 'he does')

Criticisms of Brown's work

- The study sample was restricted to three children.
- He did not account for meaning, but only looked at the length of what was said.
- His framework cannot be used to measure the clarity of speech.

Criticisms of Chomsky's LAD

- Lack of scientific evidence to support theory.
- Does not explain the importance of the environment (**nurture**) in language development.
- Does not take into account the role of adults in supporting language development.
- He emphasised the importance of grammar in sentence development, rather than meaning.

Now try this

Give **two** reasons why you should not 'overcorrect' children's language. Refer to Chomsky's LAD and Brown's stages.

Bruner

Jerome Bruner's **theory of development** is based on the concept of a 'spiral curriculum' in which children can be helped to develop new ideas at a basic level. These are revisited and gradually become more complex.

Bruner's Language Acquisition Support System (LASS)

Bruner observed that:

- children need social interaction to develop cognitive and language skills
- a language-rich environment is essential for children's language development
- adults facilitate language acquisition, a process he referred to as 'scaffolding'.

Bruner used the **Language Acquisition Support System** (LASS) to describe the development of language.

Scaffolding learning

Scaffolding describes the process of supporting children in their learning to help them reach the next level of cognitive and language development. It is based on, and similar to, Vygotsky's Zone of Proximal Development (ZPD).

Examples of scaffolding in practice include:

- ✓ simplifying language
- ✓ motivating children
- ✓ modelling language.

🔗 **Links** To revise more about Vygotsky see page 55.

Representation

Bruner identified three **modes of representation** to describe the ways in which we learn. We learn by storing and encoding information.

1   **Enactive representation** – learning through physical actions. **Information** is gained through hands-on activity and is stored in children's memories.

2   **Iconic representation** – image-based learning whereby children use one thing to represent another. **Pictures** used alongside words help children to store visual images.

3   **Symbolic representation** – using and understanding abstract symbols to represent ideas. Children **interpret symbols** (words) to form a mental picture.

Children learn new things and form memories through hands-on experiences.

LAD and LASS differences

Chomsky's Language Acquisition Device (**LAD**) differs from Bruner's Language Acquisition Support System (**LASS**).

- ✓ **Chomsky** believed language acquisition was predetermined; that children's brains are 'pre-wired' for learning language and the environment has little impact.
- ✓ **Bruner** believed that the environment, with opportunities for social interaction, is essential for children's language development.

Now try this

Emily is 3 years old. At nursery she is reluctant to socialise with other children and finds difficulty in following instructions. Her speech is delayed and she only strings two or three words together.

Suggest **three** ways in which her key worker could 'scaffold' Emily to develop her speech, language and communication.

Vygotsky

Lev Vygotsky believed social interaction with adults and other children is essential for cognitive and language development. For this reason, Vygotsky's **constructivist learning theory** is sometimes referred to as social constructivist learning theory.

Language development

Vygotsky viewed children as '**apprentices**' who learn from others. The following four points help to explain how children develop language skills, according to Vygotsky:

Links Vygotsky is also revised as part of Unit 1 on page 17. If you have already revised this within Unit 1, complete the 'Now try this' to test your revision.

1 Language learning is an active process.

2 The development of language is the result of social interaction.

3 Children are apprentices who learn language from others.

4 Language is important for cognitive development.

Vygotsky's Zone of Proximal Development (ZPD)

Vygotsky believed that children could master skills with support and guidance, which they could not do alone. He called this the Zone of Proximal Development (ZPD).

The child's actual development | The child's potential development

Zone of Actual Development (ZAD)	Zone of Proximal Development (ZPD)	
What children know and can do independently	What children can achieve with support from an adult or child with higher level knowledge and skills	What children are unable to understand or do even with support

Increasing task difficulty ⟶

Types of speech

Vygotsky differentiated between **social speech** and **private speech**.

✓ **Social speech** is used by children to communicate with others.

✓ **Private speech** is directed to the self and used for self-direction. Children use it in play and it helps to develop their thought processes.

Vygotsky believed thought and language are separate systems until around the age of 3 years.

Supporting speech

In your practice, supporting speech means:

- **using close observation** of children's current development to inform planning for their next steps (ZPD)
- **using questioning and modelling language** to develop children's language skills
- **giving opportunities for exploration and play** to develop private speech.

Now try this

Ajay is playing with the posting box but is not yet able to find the correct shape to 'post' in the square hole. His key person picks up the cube and demonstrates how to place it in the hole. He takes it out and passes it to Ajay who then posts it himself.

How does Vygotsky's ZPD theory help to explain the key person's interaction with Ajay?

Piaget

Jean Piaget believed that children pass through four distinct developmental stages of learning.

4 Formal operations: from 11 up to 18 years:
Young people have the ability for abstract thoughts, rational thought and problem solving.

3 Concrete operations: from 7 to 11 years:
Children use practical resources to help them to understand the world, such as counters for mathematics. They classify, categorise and use logic to understand things they see.

2 Pre-operational: from 2 to 7 years:
Children begin to control their environment by using symbolic behaviour, including representational words and drawings and pretend play, but are not yet able to think logically.

1 Sensorimotor: from birth to 2 years:
Infants learn about their environment and develop early schemas (concepts) by using all their senses to physically explore the world.

Piaget's stages of learning

Piaget's constructivist theory

Piaget's theory is based on four suppositions.

1 Children are **active learners**.

2 Children **think differently** from **adults**.

3 Children **construct their own meanings** from their experiences and the environment around them.

4 Language depends on the **development of thought** – cognition before language.

Application

How can constructivist theory be applied to your practice?

- Provide activities that reflect children's stage of cognitive development.
- Plan opportunities for exploratory play to enable children to develop their thoughts, which will lead to language development.

Vygotsky and Bruner differences

Here are four ways in which Vygotsky and Bruner's theories differ from Piaget's. According to Vygotsky and Bruner:

- language development is a social process, so it is referred to as social constructivism
- the role of adults is critical for facilitating language and cognitive development
- cognition is driven by language development, rather than language by cognition
- with support, children can progress more quickly than Piaget suggests in his stages

Now try this

Describe what may be happening in the photo, with reference to Piaget's constructivist theory.

Factors affecting communication

Personal and environmental factors may affect speech, language and communication, creating barriers to communication.

Children need a quiet area where distractions are reduced, to take part in effective communication.

Background noise
Background noise affects a child's ability to tune in to their parent's or key person's voice.

Excessive use of screens
Tablets and TVs inhibit social interaction, which is critical for speech and language development.

Learning difficulties
Learning difficulties can cause speech delay and difficulty in learning the 'rules' of language:
- **expressive** – using the right words and grammar, pronouncing words correctly
- **receptive** – listening and following instructions.

Factors that may affect speech, language and communication

Conductive hearing loss

The quality of adult interaction
Effective child–adult interactions involve:
- responding to babies' vocalisations
- modelling language
- using positive non-verbal interactions, such as eye contact, body language, gesture.

Conductive hearing loss

This condition:

☑ is common in children between 2 years and 6 years

☑ prevents sounds passing between the eardrum and the inner ear

☑ is often caused by fluid build-up behind the eardrum (glue ear) and ear infections.

Links Conductive hearing loss is also revised in the context of additional needs on page 85.

Inner ear   Middle ear   Outer ear

Eardrum

Conductive hearing loss can affect speech, communication and language development.

Now try this

Think about the environment and verbal and non-verbal communication.

Outline what early years practitioners can do to support children with conductive hearing loss.

Observing and assessing

Observing and assessing progress in speech, language and communication enables **early detection** of problems so that suitable **recommendations** and **referrals** can be put in place.

Difficulties in pronunciation

Ability to organise thoughts to produce words and sentences

Delays in speech

Phonological awareness

To monitor and assess speech, language and communication development, consider:

Difficulties in concentration

Ability to socialise and 'read' non-verbal communication

Ability to respond to questions

Ability to follow instructions

Hearing tests

Routine audiology tests take place shortly after birth, at around 8–12 months, and at 4–5 years to identify hearing problems. Further tests are carried out if concerns are raised about speech, communication and language development.

Identifying problems

You must understand the stages of speech, communication and language development so that you recognise when a child is displaying typical behaviour for their stage of development and when they are experiencing difficulties.

Early recognition of problems is important for:

- planning referrals and support
- identifying hearing problems or learning difficulties
- reducing the long-term impact of problems.

Not recognising problems can lead to:

- lack of progression in areas of the curriculum
- delays in cognitive development
- socialisation and behavioural problems.

Now try this

Give **three** aspects of children's speech, language and communication skills that might be observed and assessed during social play.

Consider the importance of observing both verbal speech and non-verbal communication.

Babies and speech

Social interaction in the first year of life provides a foundation for language development.

Pre-linguistic stage

This stage is from birth to around 12–13 months. Babies need to tune in to language. To be able to do this, they must spend time with their main carer and/or key worker.

Birth–2 months

Uses vocalisations to express feelings and needs, and will turn head toward the source of a noise

2–6 months

Responds with babbling and cooing, and shows feelings through facial expressions

7–8 months

Uses repeated sounds such as 'da da', 'ba ba' to respond to adult interaction

10+ months

Understands around 20 words and will point to objects when asked

Interaction with babies

You need to know about the four types of **early interaction** with babies.

 Drawing babies' attention

Babies' attention can be gained by getting close and facing them, and minimising any distractions. Using commentary on what is happening helps babies to focus and engage with the adult.

 Gesture

Pointing to objects when naming helps babies to understand words before they can say them. Gestures help babies to focus on objects, people or actions.

 Facial expression

Before language, babies learn to 'read' and copy facial expressions. They will be drawn to the movements of mouths, eyes and eyebrows, and communicate their own feelings through their face.

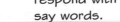 **Eye contact**

Gaining eye contact is critical for effective communication with babies. They focus on the sounds and facial expressions and will respond with sounds even before they can say words.

Parentese

This style of language, used by mothers and fathers, was observed by researchers in the 1970s. It is considered to aid babies' understanding. Speech patterns in parentese involve:

- simplified language
- higher pitched sounds
- repetition.

Early language

In your practice this means:

- planning and using opportunities for communicating with babies throughout the day
- interacting socially to encourage babies to use sounds and gestures
- acting as the key person for a baby to build a strong attachment.

> **Now try this**
>
> Fariq is 10 months old. Suggest **two** activities to support and develop Fariq's speech, communication and language.

Effective environments

Effective language environments provide suitable **space**, **time** and **resources** to encourage speaking and listening.

Characteristics of an environment that promotes language

 Layout

Provide layouts that promote language development, for example:

- soft seating areas for sharing books, stories and language games
- areas for role play and imaginative play, e.g. home corner, dens or tents
- avoid making spaces where children are disturbed by others passing though.

A layout with small spaces where children will not be disturbed encourages language use and concentration.

 Activities and resources

Well-planned activities will engage and excite children, leading to the development of ideas that they will express through their play and interactions.

- Plan activities and resources that are age/stage appropriate.
- Vary resources to keep children's interest and extend vocabulary.
- Add new resources during play to maintain interest.

 Noise

Keep noise levels low to encourage children to vocalise and to reduce the likelihood of distraction.

- Model low-volume but clear speech.
- Provide quiet areas.
- Avoid continuous background noise or loud music.
- Do not call out across the room.

Some activities, such as story time, puppets and imaginative play, are particularly good for promoting language.

 Group size

Group size determines the amount and type of interaction children have with other children and with significant adults.

- Use small groups that give the opportunity for more effective social interaction.
- Use careful grouping to ensure that children can learn from each other and no one child dominates the discussion.
- Consider age and stage of development when grouping children.

Now try this

Draw a plan of your own setting and label it. On the plan, identify any positive characteristics that encourage language development.

Promoting language

Your skills in **supporting** and **responding** to children make a difference to their speech, language and communication development.

Active listening
- positive body language
- using eye contact
- responding to talk
- reflecting back
- smiling and nodding

Encouraging talk
- introduce new and interesting things to talk about
- ask questions
- give time to respond
- give praise
- model language
- use accurate vocabulary and grammar

Ways to promote language development

Sequencing
- help children to order their ideas to form their sentences
- prompt children to retell their experiences

Drawing attention to detail
- talk about actions and objects
- expand on children's vocabulary

Accurate naming
- point to objects while naming
- introduce more accurate naming words as children's language develops

Links To revise Vygotsky's constructivist learning theory and remind yourself of what he said about the importance of social interaction, see page 55.

Overcorrecting

Don't overcorrect children's attempts at language as this discourages them from speaking.

> I wented to the park.

> You went to the park? How nice!

Model correct forms of language when using **active listening** techniques. Remember, getting the tense wrong or mispronouncing words is a normal part of the language development process.

Now try this

Identify **three** opportunities in the day at your own setting when you can give time to encourage children to talk.

One example would be at mealtimes – think of three more opportunities.

Reading and writing skills

Even before children are ready to read, it is important to introduce them to written material, so that they can acquire the reading and writing skills they will need.

Developing reading skills

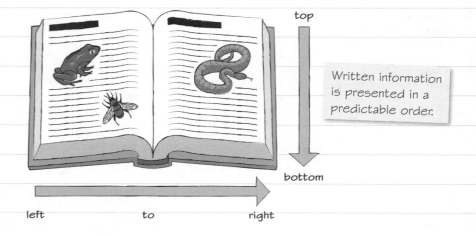

Understand the direction of reading (for example, reading and writing from left to right, and top to bottom)

Know how to handle books and other written material (holding books and turning pages)

Knowledge and skills for reading

Know how to use interactive computer programs (responding to information on a screen and manipulating using touch or a mouse)

Use spoken language fluently

top

bottom

left   to   right

Written information is presented in a predictable order.

Supporting reading and writing skills

You need to know how to support these three essential reading and writing skills.

1 **Link sounds with the written symbol**

Share books, play matching games and carry out writing activities.

2 **Recognise letters and written symbols**

Help children to distinguish between pictures and words. Point to and say initial sounds in words.

3 **Understand simple sentence structures**

Point to words while reading sentences. Enable children to 'read along' with familiar or repetitive stories.

Now try this

Make a list of reading materials (to include books, games and interactive software) that you could use with children at different ages and stages. Note **two** skills that could be developed through sharing each one.

Sort materials into those that are suitable for babies up to 1 year, children from 1 to 3 years, and children from 4 to 5 years. This will help you to select materials for your set task.

Language-rich environment

A language-rich environment helps to promote children's curiosity in the written word and an interest in books and materials.

Making a language-rich environment

You need to know how to build a language-rich environment using the four strategies shown below.

 Labelled displays

Labelled displays help children to link words to pictures and symbols.

Examples in practice

- Label children's artwork.
- Label displays with key words from current topics.
- Label resources so children can link the word shape to the object.

② **Word banks**

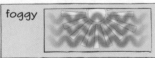 

Today the weather is

_____

Children become familiar with the shape of common words.

③ **Labelling activities**

Labelling activities help children to create links in an active and involved way.

Examples in practice

- Place the child's own name next to their choices, e.g. activities, food preferences.
- Match topic words to pictures or objects on a table display.
- Add the child's own name to their work.

Examples in practice

- Display words that children use regularly, to build their **sight vocabulary**.
- Give easy access to words so that children can select and use them in their writing.
- Get children to make and display their own word lists.

④ **Areas for reading and writing**

Dedicated small spaces help excite children's interest to focus on reading and writing.

Examples in practice

- Provide attractive and quiet areas to encourage small groups of children to become absorbed in their literacy activities.
- Provide comfortable seating.
- Provide a wide range of reading and writing materials.
- Organise areas to enable children to select (and return) reading or writing materials.

A language environment

Things to remember when planning.

- ✓ Words must be at children's eye level.
- ✓ Words should be written clearly, using the font of the setting.
- ✓ Involve children in labelling and using labels and words.
- ✓ Model ways to interact with your literacy environment.

Now try this

Identify **five** characteristics of a language-rich environment.

Phonemic awareness

Children learn to read by developing their phonemic awareness (hearing the sounds) and making links to graphemes (groups of letters/written symbols).

Books, playing and reading

Sharing books and playing literacy games helps children to develop the skills required for reading. Children need experiences to develop the following skills.

 Recognition of individual speech sounds

CAT — 'c' makes the sound /k/ in speech

> Children learn to recognise individual letters or groups of letters that represent sounds in speech.

CHURCH — 'c' and 'h' together make one sound, /ch/

2 **Ability to segment words into their component phonemes**

Children learn to segment words into their component parts for reading, and to blend phonemes to spell and write words. For example, they start with consonants and vowels in simple words ('c', 'a' and 't') and move on to blends like /c/, /l/, /a/, /p/.

3 **Ability to link phonemes with graphemes**

duckling

> Children learn to link spoken sounds (**phonemes**) with written symbols (**graphemes**).

Early literacy

Children's early literacy is developed through their experiences and senses.

✓ **Touch** – pointing to words, holding magnetic or solid letter shapes.

✓ **Sight** – using pictures that link with words.

✓ **Hearing** – listening to the sounds while pointing to the written letter or word.

Phonemic awareness

In your practice:

- introduce sounds in order of usefulness; not alphabetical order
- say sounds (phonemes) while pointing to symbols (graphemes) when sharing books and literacy games
- say each sound clearly and correctly – for example, a short /t/, not /tuh/ or /tee/.

Now try this

Identify **two** activities for children who are developing their reading. These activities should help them to link sounds (phonemes) to symbols (graphemes).

Reading development

Stories and rhymes are a fun way to introduce the skills required for early reading.

Introducing reading skills

Reading skills can be introduced to children by:

- using stories and rhyme recognition
- linking pictures and words to actions that carry meaning.

Sharing stories and rhymes

Encourage children to join in with the rhyme at the end of the sentence.

Talk about what is happening in each part of the picture and point to the words that tell you.

Incy Wincy Spider climbed up the water spout, down came the rain and washed the spider out

Out came the sun and dried up all the rain, so Incy Wincy Spider climed up the spout again!

Talk about the words on the page. 'Which word is "up"?' 'Which word is "down"?' 'What might happen to the spider?'

Ask children what they think is happening in the picture.

Stories and rhymes that are suitable for young children introduce repetition of sounds, words and rhythms that are easy to copy.

Stories and rhymes

In your practice:

- make sure children are close, settled and will not be distracted
- read in a playful way
- use a rhythmic voice that children can join in with
- get children to join in with actions to help memory.

Now try this

Choose a rhyme for use with a group of 3-year-olds.

(a) Plan how you would use the rhyme.

(b) Identify **three** literacy skills that could be developed.

Literacy support

There are many opportunities for supporting the development of literacy skills in early years settings.

Coming together for circle time gives children the opportunity to listen to others and to express their own ideas and feelings.

Puppet play encourages speech through the ordering and retelling of stories. Children's ideas are also often recorded in drawings, mark making and writing.

Experiencing rhythm and rhyme, and learning lyrics develops **auditory discrimination**.

Cutting and sticking, choosing materials and talking about work all develop language. Children also develop **fine motor skills** required for writing.

As children play with small-world toys, such as dolls houses and farm animals, they often use **commentary** on their actions, developing speech and vocabulary.

A storytelling area encourages children to share books, read alone or listen to recorded stories.

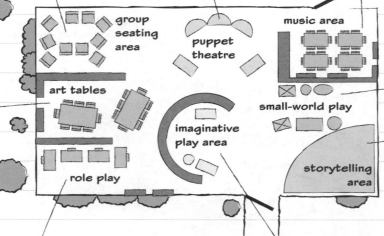

Role play enables children to practise listening and speaking, using language to communicate, sharing and negotiating. Writing and reading is developed by 'play writing' activities, such as making shopping lists and filling in appointment books.

In imaginative play, children use speech to make up storylines, they negotiate roles and often retell and record their actions in their mark making and writing.

Children often provide commentary on their own play and activity as they develop their literacy skills.

Links To revise what Vygotsky describes as **social speech** and **private speech**, see page 55.

Story sacks

When storytelling, using cloth bags as story sacks that contain objects and materials relating to the story:

- helps to stimulate speech and language
- allows children to link objects shown to the written and spoken words
- aids memory to help children to order and retell stories in pictures or writing.

Now try this

Your manager has asked you to prepare a story sack for the story 'The Three Bears' to use with a group of 3-year-olds. List the resources you could place in the sack.

Theoretical approaches

Synthetic phonics is commonly used in the development of reading and writing. This approach is often combined with other approaches.

Combining approaches

Here are four approaches to help children learn to read.

 Synthetic phonics

This approach is commonly used in schools. The **advantages** are that children are introduced to **phonemes** (sounds) and associated **graphemes** (written letters) are taught individually. Children use this knowledge to segment words, starting with simple consonant-vowel-consonant (CVC) words like c-a-t. Initially, children are introduced to the common letter sounds (/s/, /a/, /t/, /l/, /p/, /n/) and then to groups of letters that form one sound (such as /oa/), until they know all 44 phonemes in the English language. **Systematic synthetic phonics** describes the approach when used as a teaching framework.

Disadvantages

- The technique does not help understanding of the meaning of words.
- Some words cannot be segmented in this way.

 Analytical phonics

This approach emphasises the initial letter sound (unlike the synthetic phonics approach, which emphasises each part of the word). Children do not pronounce sounds in isolation, but learn about sounds in words they come across. The **advantages** are that children are introduced to common phonemes so they can apply them as they read, for example 'cake', 'make' or 'lake'.

Disadvantage

- Many English words do not follow a pattern, but there are many words that children need to recognise by shape.

 Whole language/apprenticeship approach

This approach follows the constructivist theory of learning. The **advantages** are that children learn to read by experiencing books and making sense of the words they read. It is based on a belief that language should not be broken down into separate sounds to decode or segment words. Children should learn to understand words in relation to each other and in the context of the story.

Disadvantage

- Some children, especially those with reading difficulties, benefit from strategies to break down words to support their reading.

 Look and say

This approach is similar to the whole-language approach. Children learn words by sight as whole units. The **advantage** of this approach is that children learn words next to pictures, so make an association which helps them to remember them. Children eventually learn to recognise the shapes of words, and gradually build up their sight vocabulary.

Disadvantages

- Children rely on memory to read.
- It does not help them to tackle new words.

Holding and using a book correctly   Reading with expression

Saying sounds aloud when writing words

Modelling literacy skills promotes reading development and integrates practical and theoretical approaches

Demonstrating strategies for reading difficult words

Acting as scribe

Explaining the meaning of text

Joining in writing activities   Predicting what might happen next

---

Now try this

Suggest an activity that you could use to support the reading development of children in three different age ranges. Justify your choice of activity and its appropriateness for each group.

Reading sequence

For the majority of children, learning to read follows a similar sequence. The skills outlined here are essential for effective reading development.

Reading readiness

1 **Recognising the link between the verbal and visual word** – knowing that spoken words can be shown as written symbols.

↓

2 **Recognising own name** – pointing out their own written name.

↓

3 **Using picture cues** – looking at pictures to deduce what words and sentences might say.

↓

4 **Understanding and using book conventions** – knowing how to turn pages and knowing direction of text (e.g. running from left to right and from top to bottom).

↓

5 **Phonetic awareness** – having an understanding of printed letters and knowing they stand for sounds.

↓

6 **Retelling stories** – being able to say what happened first, in the middle and at end of a story.

↓

7 **Acquisition of high-frequency words** – building a visual knowledge of words they see frequently.

↓

Ready for reading

Support for reading

In your assessment task you may have to consider ways that adults support children's reading and/ or produce plans for literacy activities. The following are strategies that can be used to support the development of reading skills.

- ✓ Make reading a fun, positive experience.
- ✓ Give lots of opportunity for handling and sharing books.
- ✓ Play literacy games.
- ✓ Produce sounds correctly and clearly for children to copy.
- ✓ Point out words in the environment.
- ✓ Praise attempts to make sounds or read words.
- ✓ Talk about the text when reading.
- ✓ Ask open-ended questions to encourage the use of picture cues.
- ✓ Display age/stage-appropriate common, or high-frequency words.

Now try this

1 Produce a list of common words that might be found in story books for children aged 5 years.
2 Suggest **two** activities that can be used with children to build their visual memory of common words.

Choosing books for different stages

You may choose books to use with children with a specific purpose or activity in mind. It is also important that children have the opportunity to choose their own books. Children enjoy books and like to participate.

Books should be varied and reflect children's interests and stage of development.

Birth to 2 years

Babies enjoy books, using all their senses to explore them. They recognise and can point to pictures. They can make sounds, for example, of animals they see, and around the age of 12 months are beginning to name pictures.

Suitable books include:

- picture books
- board and cloth books
- interactive books
- books with colourful pictures
- books with recognisable pictures.

3–5 years

Children are beginning to develop **early reading skills**. They can recognise the shapes of some words, know the names and sounds of some letters, are beginning to **segment** words to read and can link words to pictures.

Suitable books include:

- stories with pictures and linking words
- books with simple story plots
- storylines that children can identify with
- books with repetition, rhythmic language and rhyme
- fun books, such as pop-up books
- **non-fiction** titles about familiar topics.

6–8 years

Children are beginning to be competent readers. They can segment words, recognise familiar words and use what they know about sentence structure, the flow of language and illustrations to work out unfamiliar words. Children enjoy interesting story plots, and can remember and retell them, using their imagination to predict what might happen.

Suitable books include:

- stories with some illustration
- non-fiction books with themes and information that encourage discussion
- more complex plots and storylines
- books appropriate to the child's reading age
- books from favourite authors.

Now try this

Select one book to use with each of the three age groups, giving reasons for your choice.

Literacy experiences

As well as using books, there are many other activities that help children to develop literacy skills in early years settings.

Matching activities

Matching games help to develop different types of literacy skills.

Activities	Skills
• Picture or word lotto • Matching pictures • Picture dominoes • Jigsaw puzzles	**Visual discrimination** – looking at pictures supports eventual discrimination of letter and word shapes
• Sound snap • Sound lotto • Rhyming dominoes • Games that identify sounds	**Auditory discrimination** – Identifying/recognising beginning and ending letter sounds and recognition of rhyming words
• Word or picture lotto • Word-building cards • Jigsaw puzzles	**Decoding**, **segmenting** and **blending** words
• Word dominoes • Word snap • Word bingo	**Recognition** – of common words and irregular words that cannot be segmented and blended

Big books

Use big books so that all the children can see the picture and follow the text.

Group story time

Reading in a group develops a variety of skills.
- Choose stories at an appropriate interest level.
- Make sure that children are comfortable and can see the book easily.
- Use visual cues and props to help children to follow the text.
- Demonstrate skills in turning pages, and in the reading direction – reading from left to right and from top to bottom.
- Help children to identify the main events in the story.
- Demonstrate ways to segment and blend words.
- Draw attention to rhyming words.

Now try this

Identify **three** ways in which this professional could use the activity of sharing a story to develop children's reading skills.

This early years professional is sharing a story with a group of 3-year-olds.

Sharing books

Sharing books and stories is a key way of developing reading skills and a love of reading. Books can also be used as inspiration to develop ideas for children's pictures, mark making and writing.

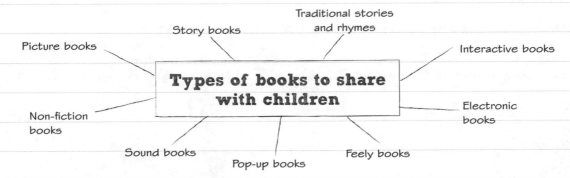

Picture books

Story books

Traditional stories and rhymes

Interactive books

Types of books to share with children

Non-fiction books

Electronic books

Sound books

Pop-up books

Feely books

Why are books important?

Sharing books:

- ✓ **introduces** reading skills in a fun way
- ✓ **extends** vocabulary
- ✓ **captures** children's interest in reading
- ✓ **supports** auditory discrimination
- ✓ **encourages** speech.

Children who enjoy sharing books at a very young age are more likely to develop into competent readers.

Auditory discrimination

Auditory discrimination describes how the brain distinguishes between different sounds to produce speech. Speech production is essential for developing phonological awareness. You can help children to discriminate between sounds and to produce them in their speech by using stories and rhymes that have:

- **repetition** – this helps children to tune in to sounds and encourages participation
- **rhythm** – encourages children to engage with the story, remember words and develop speech patterns
- **rhyming words** – these help children to tune in to the end sounds in words.

Now try this

Eleanor works in a nursery with children aged 2 to 3 years. She has been asked to plan an activity to support a group of three children to tune in to sounds. One of the children has delayed language development.

In your set task, you may have to plan for a specific age group and/or for children with specific literacy needs.

Select a traditional story or rhyme that would be suitable for this age group. Plan ways to encourage participation from all the children.

Handwriting

Handwriting is different from writing. The development of handwriting depends on **fine motor skills** which, as they develop, enable children to control and coordinate movement of the small muscles in fingers and hands.

Writing skills - from mark making to handwriting

 Palmar grip
(developing at around 12 months)

The crayon is held vertically. The child moves their whole arm to make marks on paper.

 Simple tripod grip
(developing at around 3.5 years)

Children use the whole pads of the fingers against the pencil. They move their wrists, but continue to use their arms. At this stage, a child is able to draw and make shapes using a chunky crayon.

 Digital grip
(developing at around 2-3 years)

The pencil is held with the index finger pointing down to the point of the pencil, giving the child more control to make dots and circles.

 Tripod grip
(developing at around 5-6 years)

Children use their fingertips with the pencil held at an angle. Finger and wrist movements are better controlled, enabling children to form letters correctly. By around 7 years old, children are able to form joined-up letters.

Left-handedness

Young children may not develop handedness until the age of 3 to 4 years. Writing can be more difficult for left-handed children as they have to push the pencil, rather than pull it across the sheet of paper. It is important to help them develop a comfortable writing position.

You can support left-handed children by:
- providing a triangular pencil or a rubber grip that fits on the pencil
- helping them to adopt a tripod grip
- placing the paper at an angle – rotating it clockwise by about 45 degrees
- seating the child to the left of a right-handed child, so they do not bump each other.

Now try this

Observe three children at different ages and note down the type of writing grip they use.

In your set task, you may be asked to identify appropriate mark making or writing materials that are suitable for children at a particular age or stage of writing.

Writing development

Writing depends on the development of fine motor skills and on an understanding that words carry meaning.

Early experiences

As soon as children can hold a crayon, they will start to make simple marks on paper: lines, circles and dots.

Writing development

When children begin to understand that sounds (phonemes) can be written down (graphemes), they start to include recognisable letter shapes in their drawings. Children will be able to tell you what their marks mean before you are able to decipher them. Their writing is a representation of their thoughts and experiences.

Letters — Shopping lists — Making cards

Writing for purpose

Posters — Labels — Recipes

Handwriting

You can support handwriting development by:

- modelling writing
- helping children to hold the pencil correctly
- practising shaping letters with a finger
- teaching letters with the same formation in sequence, e.g. 'c', then 'a', then 'd'
- using a start point and arrow cues to show how to start and form the letter.

Support for writing

Providing large areas for painting and drawing gives children opportunities to develop their writing skills.

Now try this

Give **three** reasons why it is important to support handwriting skills alongside writing development.

Writing sequence

The sequence of writing development depends on cognitive development. As children's phonemic awareness and their understanding of sentence structure develop, children become increasingly confident in recording their ideas.

Writing development

1 **At around 1–2 years old**, children enjoy making **simple marks** on paper: lines, circles or dots.

2 **By around 3 years old**, children begin to understand that writing **carries meaning**. Alongside their pictures, they begin to form shapes or symbols and can talk about what their writing means.

> In this sample, the child is starting to form shapes that represent curved letter shapes.

3 **By around 4 years**, children develop **phonemic awareness** and use their knowledge to write words. They know how to spell their name and include it in their writing.

> In this sample, the letters are well formed, although they vary in size. The work shows an awareness of sounds. This child would be able to 'read' their own writing.

4 **By around 5 years**, children begin to **segment** and **blend sounds** to spell common and simple words. Children can form their ideas to produce simple coherent sentences. They start to use capital letters and full stops.

> In this sample, words are now spaced and letters are formed correctly, but the height of letters is inconsistent.

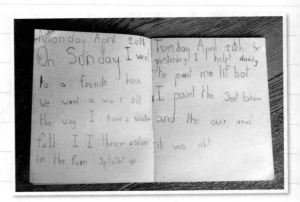

5 **By 6–8 years old**, children develop ideas and can **structure their writing** for different purposes, such as lists, letters or stories with a beginning, middle and end. Their letters are joined and are of consistent size.

Now try this

Give **three** activities that can help a child aged 4 years to form letter shapes.

Writing and reading

Many of the play activities that take place in early years settings support the development of both reading and writing.

> Activities supporting links between reading and writing help to develop children as confident readers and writers.

Role play

Realistic writing situations help to develop children's reading. You could provide materials for note taking, making lists, writing letters and making cards.

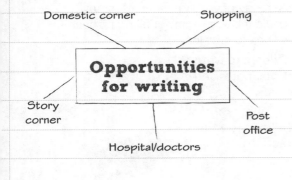

Stories and drama

Opportunities for speaking, listening and reading are important for inspiring the writing process. You could encourage children to join in activities, draw out rhythms and rhymes in language (spoken and sung) and order pictures to tell the events in a story. You could also use writing activities such as posters, letters and cards based on story or drama.

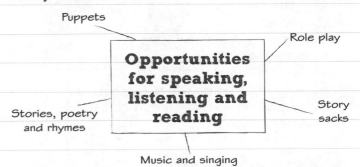

Creative play

In creative play, including making music, children develop the fine motor skills and hand–eye coordination that they need for writing. They also develop visual discrimination. You could provide finger painting for early mark making, printing blocks, collage for cutting and sticking, a painting wall and musical instruments.

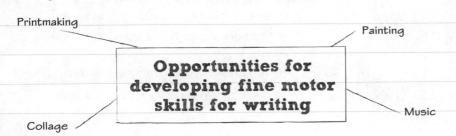

Sand play

In addition to sand play being fun, it is a useful medium for the development of reading and writing. You could show children how to write letter shapes in the sand with their fingers or sticks, or play at hiding, finding and recognising plastic letter shapes.

Now try this

Select a story for a story-themed activity area. Identify resources that could be provided to support and link writing and reading development.

Literacy and home

Working closely with parents and carers is important in supporting the development of children's literacy. Sharing literacy activities in this way enhances children's interest and enjoyment.

Run information sessions on developing children's literacy

Suggest lists of books and literacy ideas

Ways for you to work with parents and carers

Loan books and word games

Provide leaflets and posters to encourage parents and carers to get involved

Teach parents and carers literacy games to play with their children

Tips for parents on ways to support their  children

1 Speaking and listening

- Use different times in the day for talking, such as meal times or even when changing baby's nappy.
- Use puppets to encourage children to respond to questions. This works well with shy children.
- Use time on the way to school, on a bus or in the car to ask open-ended questions that start a discussion.

3 Writing

- Keep a range of writing materials handy. This could include forms for filling in, post-it notes and old envelopes.
- Ask children to write thank-you notes and postcards.
- Display photos and get children to write the captions.

2 Sharing books

- Set aside time every day to share a story.
- Have a variety of reading materials at home, including stories, non-fiction and comics.
- Talk about the pictures in a story and point out words that link to them.
- Encourage children to join in with rhymes and repeating parts of the story.
- Join the local library.

4 Reading

- Let children see you reading for information and pleasure.
- Point out words on the way to school or in the supermarket.
- Play word games, such as snap, word bingo and I spy.
- Write fun messages with magnetic letters.

Now try this

Naomi is 3 years old. She has language delay and is reluctant to join in at story time. Suggest ways that Naomi's key person can work in partnership with her parents to develop her language skills.

Mathematical experiences

Early hands-on play and learning experiences help children to prepare for each component of the mathematics curriculum, including numeracy.

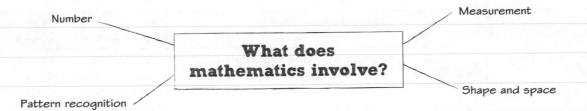

Number

Pattern recognition

What does mathematics involve?

Measurement

Shape and space

Early mathematical skills

You need to know how children's developing skills relate to the four components of early years mathematics.

1 **Number**

- Counting from 1 to 20
- Counting on or back
- Ordering, e.g. by size or colour
- Knowing more or less
- Adding and subtracting single-digit numbers, doubling, sharing and halving

2 **Measurement**

- **Size** – comparing and measuring height or length
- **Weight** – balancing, heavier than and lighter than
- **Capacity** – pouring, identifying more and less, full or empty
- **Time** – understanding o'clock
- **Money** – recognising, counting and using coins

3 **Shape and space**

- Understanding the difference between 2D shapes and 3D shapes
- Knowing about position and distance
- Sorting objects by shape and size
- Knowing the characteristics of shapes, e.g. flat, curved

4 **Pattern recognition**

- Recognising, describing and creating a pattern
- Completing a repeating pattern

Now try this

Here are some examples of language associated with number: more than, fewer than, how many, count, share. Give examples of language associated with:

- measurement
- shape and space
- pattern recognition.

77

Mathematical support

It is important to plan for a range of **independent** play and **adult-supported activities** that give opportunities for the development of numeracy and mathematical concepts.

Supporting children's early skills

Everyday activities can support mathematical and numeracy skills. Here are seven examples.

Skill	Examples of activity	How activities develop mathematical concepts
1 Matching	Games involving identifying pictures, grouping objects that are the same, sorting objects into sets	Helps children to recognise similarities and differences, mathematical symbols; the beginning of counting numeracy.
2 Pattern making	Potato printing, colouring in shapes, decorating biscuits, threading beads	Supports ability to use and recognise patterns in mathematics.
3 Counting	Stories and number rhymes, using everyday situations, setting the table, handing out snacks, counting forwards, backwards or in twos, number games with dice	Supports early calculations, working out problems involving number; helps children to gain a sense of the size of a set; develops multiplication skills.
4 Sorting	Resources that can be sorted into easily identifiable types, shape, size (e.g. animals, transport, coloured buttons)	Supports concept of groupings, language relating to similarities and differences.
5 Ordering	Ordering numerals, placing objects or toys according to size or weight	Supports the understanding of concepts relating to measurement (e.g. bigger, heavier); develops ability to follow instructions in order.
6 Recording	Using symbols, pictures or objects to record what they find out, keeping tally, copying numerals	Helps children to work out problems, communicate ideas and think about what they have found out.
7 Sharing	Getting children to share out objects between several children, sharing out snacks, working out how many are needed for two or three children	Supports early calculations, problem solving and introduces skill of division.

Now try this

Hill Street Nursery has set up a shop for children to take part in domestic play. Identify opportunities for the development of each of the numeracy and mathematical skills listed.

Mathematical strategies

Children must be supported to develop the strategies needed for the development of early mathematical skills.

Strategies and activities

You can develop the strategies needed by using hands-on games and activities, such as helping children to develop the four essential skills below.

 Counting from 1 to 20

- Using everyday numeracy activities and class routines to encourage counting out loud (e.g. children in a group), setting the table
- Playing number games and number jigsaws
- Counting moveable objects
- Using number rhymes and encouraging children to join in with actions

 Placing in order

- Using routines for ordering, like getting children to line up in order or placing objects in order of first, second, third
- Using rhymes and songs where children can hold up numerals in order
- Sequencing solid or magnetic numerals, identifying the missing numerals
- Ordering activities according to attributes (e.g. number, size)

 Adding and subtracting single-digit numbers

- Adding together sets of objects/toys
- Using questions in everyday activities (e.g. 'We have six children and four cups. How many more cups do we need?')
- Counting on and back using a number line
- Using shop play with price labels and adding up amounts to pay
- Using snap-on cubes (e.g. make sets of 10 in different ways, take away cubes to say how many are left)

 Shape and size of 3D (solid) and 2D (flat) shapes

- Using games that get children to explore shape (e.g. identifying a shape in a feely bag)
- Sorting objects according to characteristics (e.g. objects with curved edges, ones with straight edges, solid or flat shapes)
- Using construction materials
- Using art activities such as printing with 2D shapes or 3D junk modelling

Mathematical language

It is important that children are introduced to the correct vocabulary as they take part in numeracy and mathematical activities.

Positional words
in front of   under
over   inside

Number
more   fewer   greater

Mathematical language

Measurement
larger   heavier
smaller   lighter

Shape
3D/solid   2D/flat
curved   straight

Now try this

Select a number rhyme for a small group of 3-year-olds and plan how to use it interactively, drawing on the strategies above.

Mathematical development

You need to help children make **links** between their experience and the skills they need in order to develop numeracy and mathematical language and concepts.

Selecting coins

Playing shop

Opportunities for developing mathematics by linking to experience

Till receipts

Numbers in the environment, e.g. number plates and door numbers

Counting aloud

Problem solving

You can help children to explore mathematical concepts by **posing questions**.

> How can we check which is heavier: the apple or the orange?

> We have 12 sweets. Are there enough for two each?

> How can we check how many cups of water will fill the bucket?

> How many do I need to take away so that I have seven left?

Practical activities

When planning activities for numeracy and mathematical development, consider the following.

- Is the activity practical/hands-on?
- What mathematical language can be introduced/used?
- Does it give scope for problem solving?
- Can you encourage children to predict?
- Can you promote numeracy development? (E.g. counting rhymes, board games, cooking, matching socks, setting the table, making patterns, recognising patterns in the environment.)

Computer programs

counting

matching

ordering

Pattern making

Using computers and tablets reinforces an understanding of mathematical concepts.

Now try this

Plan a measuring activity and identify opportunities for:

(a) giving a commentary on what is happening

(b) asking questions.

Supporting and assessing

Professionals need to provide sensitive and focused support during numeracy and mathematical activities in order to observe and assess progress.

Assessment

Assessment should be an ongoing process (**formative**) and take place at the end of a period of learning (**summative**). The three methods below are useful to gather information and plan ways to guide children in the development of mathematical concepts.

1   **Questioning** – using open-ended questions specific to mathematical concepts to find out children's thinking.

2   **Modelling** – used to find out what children already know and can do, to be able to support them towards their next stage of mathematical development.

3   **Observation** – watching the mathematical concepts that children exhibit during their play and learning activities.

Directing thinking

You can provide support for mathematical experiences by **questioning** and **directing** thinking.

Questioning

> You have four pencils. How many more do you need for our group of six children?

Providing commentary on what children are doing

> I see that you are printing circle shapes.

Repeating

> You have told me that you have two and need three more to make five.

Praising

> Good thinking! You have chosen the star to complete the pattern.

Modelling

Interacting with children as they play helps you to:

- understand how they think about mathematical concepts
- use a commentary to introduce and model mathematical language
- plan activities to help them to progress to the next stage
- provide additional support or explanation with children whose home language is not English or who have learning or sensory difficulties.

This early years professional is observing the mathematical concepts the child is using in a counting activity. She will use this information to inform and plan development of new concepts.

Now try this

A group of children aged 4 years are playing with different sized containers in the water.

Suggest **three** open-ended questions you could use to assess their understanding of capacity.

Mathematics and home

Working closely with parents and carers is important to support the development of children's skills in using number and mathematical thinking. Using practical activities will engage children's interest and enjoyment. Parents and carers who lack confidence in mathematics will need encouragement.

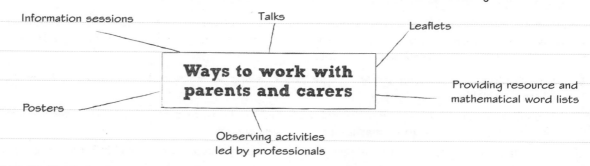

Information sessions

Talks

Leaflets

Ways to work with parents and carers

Providing resource and mathematical word lists

Posters

Observing activities led by professionals

Activities to use at home

Here are some practical and fun ways that parents and carers could use to support children's numeracy skills and development of mathematical concepts.

 Measuring

- Cooking activities – using non-standard measures and progressing to standard measures
- Counting how many strides (e.g. across the room)
- Measuring self – taller than, shorter than
- Growing seeds and measuring growth

 Shape and space

- Using and talking about building blocks
- Printing using shapes
- Colouring in pattern shapes
- Shape posting boxes

 Number

- Playing with magnetic numbers
- Counting out money when shopping
- Playing board and card games
- Looking for numbers in the street on the way to school or nursery, and identifying odd/even numbers
- Using stories and rhymes with number
- Helping with setting the table and counting plates/ spoons

 Repeated patterns

- Using beads to make a necklace
- Ordering toys (e.g. toy cars by size)
- Looking for pattern in the home – flooring/soft furnishings

Now try this

Matthew is 4 years old. He has difficulty in counting and recognising numbers to 10. Suggest **three** activities that his parents could provide at home.

Multilingualism

It is important that children are supported to learn English while at the same time recognising and valuing their home language. This gives them confidence and a sense of belonging, which promotes their self-esteem.

The context of language development

Children may be:

- confident in their home language, and learning English as a new language
- learning their home language at the same time as the English language.

Professionals must show children that they value their home language.

Stages

There are four main stages of language acquisition.

 Use of home language

Initially, children have no understanding of English. They continue to use their home language, supplemented by **gestures**.

Early years professionals should communicate using **non-verbal** methods including facial expressions and gestures alongside simple language, visual materials, pictures and artefacts.

If possible, speak (or use recordings, for example, of stories) in children's home languages. This will help children to join in all activities in the setting, which gives a positive self-image and promotes positive self-esteem.

 Non-verbal stage

As children begin to tune into English they may become reluctant to speak; this is referred to as the **silent period**.

Early years professionals should not pressurise children to talk. **Close observation** should be maintained as children are developing their understanding of words and sentences before they can speak them. **Use instructions**, such as 'give me the pencil, please', to check understanding.

 Emerging speech

Children begin to talk, but they use **formulaic speech** that they hear in the setting. They may also repeat speech that they hear. Children start to put words together to form simple sentences, although these are not always grammatically correct, such as 'me do it'.

Early years professionals should **listen actively** and provide commentary on what is happening, to give children the words to use. They should not correct children but could **recast** what has been said to model good English. Information should be simplified.

 Productive language

Children begin to **express** their ideas and feelings using sentences. They **understand** many everyday instructions and activities, but continue to **need time** to think about and formulate a response. It may take 2 to 3 years to reach this stage.

Early years professionals should provide plenty of **opportunities** to use language, including repetitive stories, word games and social play with other children who are confident in English. This helps children to store information in their long-term memory so they can retrieve it when needed. Time needs to be given for children to process information before they respond.

Now try this

Give **three** examples of ways in which a key person can support children whose home language is not English.

In your set task, you may be asked to show how you can support a child whose home language is not English.

Language learners

Until children are proficient in the language of the setting, it can be a difficult time for them. It can affect them emotionally and impact on their cognitive development.

Emotional development

If children are in an environment where they cannot understand or speak the language, it can be isolating and distressing for them. Children may experience a lack of independence if they cannot easily access routines and activities.

It is important to recognise signs of distress such as withdrawal or showing aggression towards other children.

Cognitive development

Bilingualism has cognitive advantages for children. However, until children are competent in the language of the setting, they will be at a disadvantage. They may experience regression in cognitive development and could take several years to catch up with their English-speaking peers. It is important not to make assumptions about children's stage of cognitive development simply because of their lack of English.

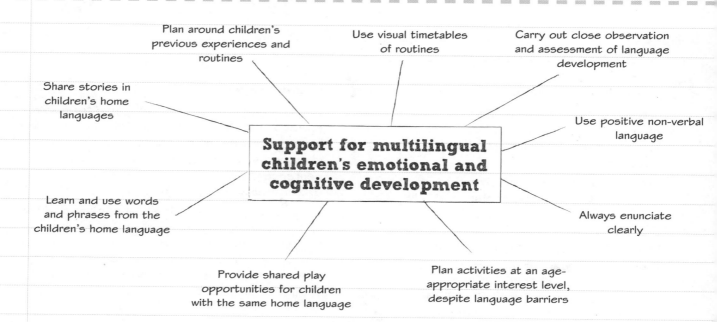

Plan around children's previous experiences and routines

Use visual timetables of routines

Carry out close observation and assessment of language development

Share stories in children's home languages

Support for multilingual children's emotional and cognitive development

Use positive non-verbal language

Learn and use words and phrases from the children's home language

Always enunciate clearly

Provide shared play opportunities for children with the same home language

Plan activities at an age-appropriate interest level, despite language barriers

Key person

The key person is important for new language learners as they:

- are the language role model
- are the first point of contact for parents
- understand children's needs and routines
- bring consistency to routines and use of language
- help children to feel safe.

Parents and carers

Close liaison with parent and carers is important for:

- understanding children's language experiences
- knowing their routines
- knowing their interests
- planning jointly to support children
- recognising problems or concerns.

Now try this

Ola is 4 years old. She has just moved to the UK from Syria with her family. Her parents speak Arabic at home and have only a little English themselves. Ola will start reception class in September.

Give **three** examples of what practitioners should do to reduce the emotional impact on Ola when she joins the reception class.

Additional needs

Children with additional needs may require carefully planned activities and specialist resources to ensure that they reach their full language potential.

Hearing loss

There are two main types of hearing loss.

 Links Conductive hearing loss is also revised in the context of factors affecting communication on page 57.

1 **Conductive hearing loss** is where sound cannot pass through the outer and inner ear to the cochlea and auditory nerve. This is often a temporary problem, which is caused by a build-up of fluid in the middle ear (glue ear).

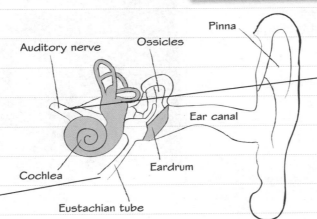

Pinna
Ossicles
Auditory nerve
Ear canal
Cochlea
Eardrum
Eustachian tube

2 **Sensori-neural hearing loss** describes hearing loss caused by damage to the nerve pathways leading from the inner ear to the brain. This type of hearing loss is usually permanent.

Speech and language delay – speech and language development follows the expected sequence but more slowly than in most children of the same age.

Speech and language disorder – language develops differently from the usual sequence of development.

Expressive language difficulties – children experience problems in using speech to express ideas.

Stammering – there is non-fluency in speech, repeating or hesitating between words.

Additional language needs

Receptive language difficulty – children have difficulties in understanding words or sentences and instructions.

Selective mutism – children are able to speak but choose not to, sometimes only in selected circumstances.

Speech difficulties – there are difficulties in articulating sounds and words.

Links To revise language acquisition see page 50, and to revise factors affecting communication, see page 57.

Signs

The following signs may indicate speech, communication or language problems.

- ✓ Lack of concentration
- ✓ Difficulty in following simple instructions
- ✓ Not responding to sounds or own name
- ✓ Difficulties in joining in play activities
- ✓ Difficulty in developing phonemic awareness compared to peers
- ✓ Unclear speech

In your set task, you may be given a case study of a child with a speech, communication and language difficulty. Understanding how this could affect them will help you to plan for their support.

Now try this

Outline the difference between speech and language delay, and speech and language disorders.

Supporting needs

Early recognition of language difficulties is important to reduce the impact on children's speech, communication and language development.

Visual cues and props

When children have communication difficulties, **visual aids** can help in making sense of routines and in communicating needs and feelings. Use:

- visual timetables
- photographs and pictures
- props and objects
- gestures and other non-verbal communication.

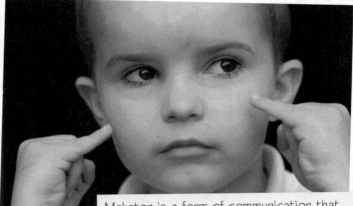

Makaton is a form of communication that uses gesture. It may be used with children with additional speech and language needs to aid their communications.

 Links To revise non-verbal communication, see page 49.

Working with parents and carers

In order to support children with additional needs, you must:

- build effective relationships with parents and carers
- find out about the child's specific needs, diagnosis and any ongoing support or treatment
- share information on the child's progress in regular meetings or calls
- work together to plan a programme of support
- use home–school diaries for two-way sharing of information on the child's activities in the setting and at home.

Build on what children already know and words they use

Give time to respond to questions and directions

Ensuring high-quality interactions to support children

Demonstrate positive body language

Provide commentary on children's play to give them access to language

Speak clearly, using simple language suitable for the child's level of development

Links To revise how activities such as imaginative play, puppets and story sacks can motivate children and support their language use, see pages 66 and 76.

Now try this

Learn five Makaton signs that could be used with children to support common routines.

Professionals in partnership

Early years practitioners must work in partnership with other professionals and parents to assess and plan to meet the needs of children with additional communication issues.

Working with others

You must understand the role of these five professionals, and how you can work with them to support children.

 Speech and language therapist

Speech and language therapists work closely with children who have speech, language and communication difficulties or disorders. They will assess the child's development and devise a programme of treatment or therapy. They may work on a one-to-one basis with the child: monitoring the child's progress, and adapting the approach or referring them to other services if necessary. They will also work with early years professionals and parents to train them to support the programme at home and in the early years setting.

You may need to work in partnership with parents and professionals from more than one service.

 Physiotherapist

Physiotherapists work with children who have physical difficulties that impact on their language and communication development. This may include supporting them to use **Makaton** to communicate or to find a suitable posture for writing. Physios give help and advice to early years professionals and often work alongside speech therapists.

Educational psychologist

Educational psychologists work with children whose speech, language and communication difficulties are a result of emotional or learning difficulties. They will consult with parents and other relevant professionals to assess the child's needs and agree a programme of support.

 Hearing support services

Hearing support services (sometimes referred to as sensory support services) are provided by the local authority. There are also charities that support children and their families. Children accessing this service will have been diagnosed by an audiologist and may have been fitted with a hearing aid or a cochlear transplant. Professionals from the hearing support service will consider the level and type of hearing loss, and how it may affect the child's developmental and learning needs. They will give advice on how best to support children, for example by speech, gesture, signing or mixed methods.

 Portage worker

Portage workers provide support for children up to 5 years old, and their families, in their own home. They give advice to parents on a number of developmental difficulties, including speech, communication and language problems. They suggest play activities and resources that will excite and interest children to make learning fun.

 Now try this

Give **three** reasons why it is important that these professionals work in partnership with early years practitioners and parents.

In your set task, you may be asked to explore how you could work with other professionals to support children with additional needs. Understanding how this could affect the children will help you to plan for their support.

Your Unit 2 set task

Unit 2 will be assessed through a task, which will be set by Pearson. You will be given activities to complete based on a case study of a fictional early years setting and a fictional case study of one or more learners from early years settings. This will assess your understanding of how children develop literacy, language, communication, numeracy and mathematical skills, and how this development is promoted and supported.

Revising your skills

Your assessed task could cover any of the essential content in the unit. You can revise the unit content in this Revision Guide. This skills section is designed to **revise skills** that might be needed in your assessed task. The section uses selected content and outcomes to provide an example of ways of applying your skills.

Reading a brief (look at a sample brief on page 89)

Relating to theories (revise this skill on page 97)

Making notes (revise this skill on page 90)

Set task skills

Recommending and justifying actions and activity plans (see pages 94–96)

Responding to case studies (see an example on page 91)

Making and justifying recommendations (see pages 92–93)

Workflow

The process of the task might involve you in making recommendations and justifying them, describing resources and roles, and linking best practice to early years theory, following these steps:

- ✓ Read the brief about a fictional early years setting
- ✓ Make notes
- ✓ Read a case study with information about issues regarding practice/provision at the setting that might relate to communication, language, literacy, numeracy, mathematical skills, then make recommendations and justify them
- ✓ Read a case study that involves one or more learners in the setting, then recommend actions for activity and justify them
- ✓ Design activities to support specific skills and needs of learners in the setting

Check the Pearson website

The activities and sample response extracts in this section are provided to help you to revise content and skills. Ask your tutor or check the Pearson website for the most up-to-date **Sample Assessment Material** and **Mark Scheme** to get an indication of the structure of your actual assessed task and what this requires of you. The details of the actual assessed task may change so always make sure you are up to date.

Now try this

Visit the Pearson website and find the page containing the course materials for BTEC National Children's Play, Learning and Development. Look at the latest Unit 2 Sample Assessment Material for an indication of:

- The structure of your set task, and whether it is divided into parts
- How much time you are allowed for the task, or different parts of the task
- What briefing or stimulus material might **be** provided to you
- Any notes you might have to make and whether you are allowed to take selected notes into your supervised assessment
- The activities you are required to complete and how to format your responses.

Reading the brief

Here are some examples of skills involved if reading a task brief on which activities in relation to children's communication, language, literacy, **numeracy** and mathematical skills are based.

Task brief

Crossdale House Nursery

Crossdale House Nursery is set in a rural area where there are a number of families who have recently sought asylum in the UK. The nursery has 34 children. Around half of the children attend the nursery full time as their parents work. Others attend either morning or afternoon sessions.

The nursery is organised into three play rooms and an outside area. The baby room currently has six infants aged between 3 months and 18 months; the toddler room has nine children aged from 19 months up to 3 years; and the pre-school room has 19 children aged from 3 years up to $4\frac{1}{2}$ years.

There are three children whose home language is not English and four children with additional learning needs.

This example is used to show the skills you need in reading a brief. The content within a task will be different each year.

Read the task brief carefully. It introduces a fictional early years setting.

Details of the setting, backgrounds of children and their families, and any language or additional needs are given.

Notice the kinds of issues involved in the setting, for example second language needs and additional learning needs of children.

 Links Activities on pages 91, 95 and 96 are based on this revision task brief.

Terms

You need to understand these terms that may be used in the activities in a task in relation to children's communication, language, literacy, numeracy and mathematical skills.

- ✓ **Activity** – a planned play and learning experience to develop child's skills and abilities.
- ✓ **Activity plan** – a structured breakdown of an experience to develop a child's skills and abilities.
- ✓ **Early years theory** – ideas that underpin early years teaching practices.
- ✓ **Resources** – pieces of equipment needed to support children's activities.

Now try this

Look again at the task brief on the crossdale House Nursey.

1 What does the task brief introduce?
2 How many children attend the nursery full time and how many attend morning or afternoon sessions?
3 How is the nursery organised?
4 What key issues are involved with some children in the setting in the brief?

Make sure you read a brief carefully and understand the information about the setting, the organisation and key issues involved with the children.

Making notes

Here are some examples of skills involved if making notes.

Key topics

Making notes on key topics may be helpful in advance of your assessment period.

- Acquisition of, and stages in, communication, literacy, numeracy and mathematical skills
- Early years theories, the differences between them, and criticisms of them
- External factors and additional needs that affect communication, literacy, numeracy and mathematical development
- Characteristics of a language-rich environment

- Role of the adult in supporting children
- Activities that support communication, literacy, numeracy and mathematics for different ages and stages
- Resources that support communication, literacy, numeracy and mathematics for different ages and stages

Structuring notes

If making notes in response to the task, you need to summarise the relevant topics quickly and in sufficient detail. Using bullet points is a useful way of keeping your notes focused and to the point.

Preparatory notes

You may be allowed to take some of your preparatory notes into your supervised assessment time. If so, there may be restrictions on the length and type of notes that are allowed. Check with your tutor or look at the most up-to-date Sample Assessment Material on the Pearson website for details.

Sample notes extract

This extract shows qualities of notes based around theories.

- Chomsky – <u>Language Acquisition Device</u> (LAD).

- Speech and language predetermined, development follows a sequence for all children.

- Does not explain delays/problems in speech.

- Unlike Vygotsky and Bruner, he thought social interaction not as critical.

- Vygotsky – **Children are apprentices.**

- Language dev't an active process that comes before cognitive dev't (opposite view to Piaget).

- Adult support helps children to reach the next stage which they would not do alone = <u>Zone of Proximal Development</u> (ZPD).

- Children use **social** speech to others and private speech to selves (e.g. commentary to self in play).

- Non-verbal communication – eye contact, gesture, body language, active listening

 Links Notes on theories can help to explain communication and literacy development. The extracts from notes given here are useful in relation to sample response extracts on page 91 and page 95.

You should write key terms in full. If you think you know them well, you could save space by writing these in brief in your notes, e.g. LAD.

You should include detail on theories that help you link them to practice. The application of theory to practice is important.

You could group similar topics together, such as highlighting for theorists, underlining for concepts, and colour for differences to help you find information easily.

Where you have a good grasp of a subject, you should only note key words as reminders.

Now try this

Identify other early years theories that support good practice and summarise the key points of each.

Responding to case studies

Here are some examples of skills involved if answering questions based on case studies.

Why are case studies important?

Case studies allow you to demonstrate your knowledge and understanding about:

- key features and stages of communication, literacy and numeracy development
- theories that help to explain communication, literacy and numeracy development
- different approaches and their impact on the promotion of communication, literacy and numeracy skills
- activities and resources to support communication, literacy and numeracy skills
- ways to provide support for children whose home language is not English and those with additional needs.

Crossdale House Nursery Review of Best Practice

Ann Shelton has just been appointed as manager of Crossdale House Nursery. Initially, she has been spending time observing and reviewing practice at the nursery. She is concerned that children's progress checks at 2 years and their Early Years Profiles at 4 years show that many children are not progressing as expected in communication and literacy. She intends to provide training for staff to:

- improve non-verbal communication skills across the staff team to develop children's speech and language
- maximise opportunities for linking reading and writing through play activities to develop literacy skills
- extend parental involvement in children's communication and literacy development.

Links This case study follows on from the task brief about Crossdale House Nursery on page 89.

The case study gives you information about issues or problems regarding practice and/ or provision at the setting, relating to communication, literacy and/or numeracy.

You need to be able to pick up clues from the case studies. This case study hints at improvements in practice, provision and engagement with parents.

With this example case study, you might be asked to produce a report that Ann could share with her staff, that:

- makes recommendations for best practice in non-verbal communication
- suggests play activities that can support reading and writing development (including guidance on adult involvement)
- justifies the suggested improvements with reference to early years theories.

Show your skills

Consider how you might respond to a case study, to:

- ✓ give recommendations to address the issues identified in the setting
- ✓ describe the resources required
- ✓ describe the role of the early years educators
- ✓ justify improvements that link best practice to early years theory
- ✓ give the response in the format required, such as a report
- ✓ notice what the bullets tell you must be included in the report and the quality of information needed – here, you must make and justify **recommendations**, not just recall your knowledge of non-verbal information.

Now try this

Produce an outline plan for the report.

Links Look at pages 92–93 to revise making recommendations and page 97 for relating to theories.

Making recommendations

Here are some examples of skills involved if you are asked to make recommendations in response to problems or issues given in a case study.

Show your skills

Consider the following qualities, using the form of a report, for example:

- ✓ **Plan** how to divide your time between the different parts of the report.
- ✓ Write an **introduction** that explains the purpose of the report – linked to the issues.
- ✓ Be aware of the **audience** – for instance, it could be early years professionals or parents.
- ✓ Be **objective**, giving reasons for your views or ideas.
- ✓ **Balance** information – consider different viewpoints or theories but don't lose **focus**.
- ✓ Use accurate **terminology** from the sector and avoid jargon.
- ✓ Reach a justified **conclusion**, referring to best practice and early years theory.

Sample response extract

The purpose of this report is to address concerns that a number of children at the nursery are not meeting their expected milestones in communication and literacy. It aims to explore how staff can develop best practice in non-verbal communication and introduce ideas for literacy activities that can improve the outcomes for all children at Crossdale House Nursery. Recommendations in this report will be supported by early years theory.

Non-verbal communication

Non-verbal communication is important for all young children as they develop their skills, but particularly for those with delayed or additional language needs. A high proportion of children's receptive and expressive language is non-verbal. It is critical, therefore, that professionals working in the nursery are aware of, and develop, effective non-verbal communication skills and use them consistently in their practice.

Eye contact

Staff should get down to a child's level and wait until there is eye contact before speaking. This reduces distractions and helps children to concentrate on and understand the information being given. It is also easier for the adult to see if the message or instruction has been understood (by observing the child's non-verbal reaction to the message, such as smiling or nodding).

Gesture

When interacting with babies, gestures such as clapping and waving encourage communication. Gesture may be used in place of speech (such as beckoning) or alongside speech when giving information or instructions. The use of gesture is important as it helps children to extend their vocabulary and to understand words or instructions. Staff should take care to use gestures that match their speech, to ensure that children do not receive mixed messages.

Links This is part of a response to the task brief on page 89 and the case study on page 91.

In this extract from a response to a case study (page 91), the learner introduces the purpose of the report with clear links to issues that have been identified in the case study.

You should use headings and sub-headings from your planning and notes. This helps you to structure the report, ensuring you include all the key information.

You should not only recall types of non-verbal communication but also give examples in practice and reasons why each is important in supporting expressive and receptive communication.

Links To revise reaching a justified conclusion see page 93, and for relating to theories see page 97.

Now try this

Extend this first section of the report by recommending ways in which **active listening** and **body language** should be used by staff. Describe how these can support children's communication.

Justifying recommendations

Here are some examples of skills involved if justifying recommendations in response to a case study. You need to show how your recommendations follow best practice, making reference to early years theories.

Sample response extract

Conclusion

Chomsky believed that children's speech and language is predetermined. He called this a Language Acquisition Device that is 'pre-wired' into the brain. However, this does not explain why some children in the nursery are falling behind in their development. Bruner and Vygotsky would argue that social interaction is essential. If, as Vygotsky believed, language development is an active process and children are 'apprentices', then the role of professionals in the setting is crucial for improving children's speech and language. Bruner's model, the Language Acquisition Support System (LASS), based on Vygotsky's theory, is helpful in explaining how adults can support children by 'scaffolding' them in their speech and language development. Using non-verbal communication is important when scaffolding as it supports children's understanding.

Piaget, Bruner and Vygotsky developed theories based on observations and research, which show that children develop language and cognition through 'hands-on' experiences. Providing well-planned play activities, such as domestic scenarios, shop play and art activities, will encourage writing and reading skills that support and promote children's literacy. Piaget's pre-operational stage describes how children engage in symbolic thought in their play. Giving opportunities for practice in writing enables children to represent their ideas through drawings, letters and words. If children have opportunities for interacting with written materials in play, such as packages in a play Post Office, they can draw on these experiences later in more formal reading and writing situations. Sensitive adult interaction, such as scribing for children as they play, will support them to develop the higher level literacy skills referred to by Vygotsky as the 'Zone of Proximal Development'. It is important, therefore, to understand each child's stage of development to be able to provide targeted support.

 Links This extract is from a conclusion to a report that justifies recommendations for improving practice. See the task brief on page 89, the case study on page 91, and making recommendations on page 92.

When writing a conclusion, reread your introduction as this outlines your initial intentions. This will help you to focus your conclusion on the correct issues.

This extract from a response gives a balanced argument. It shows understanding of weaknesses in Chomsky's LAD and gives an alternative theory to support recommendations.

You should not only recall what you know about theories, but also make justified links between theories and your recommendations for improving practice.

You do not need to define terms such as 'pre-operational' if you show that you understand what terms mean by giving examples in practice.

You should remember that literacy refers specifically to reading and writing skills.

 Links To revise theories, see Chomsky page 53, Bruner page 54, Vygotsky page 55 and Piaget page 56.

Now try this

Write another paragraph for this report linking theories to the importance of parental involvement in children's literacy development.

You could consider the role of constructivist theories that explain how experiential learning supports children's development. Discuss why this means that it is important to share ideas and practice with parents. You could also consider the role of parents in providing communication and literacy support at home, and how this links to Vygotsky's view that children can be helped to the next stage of development by an adult or older child.

Set of actions and activity plans

Here are some examples of skills involved if asked to produce a **set of actions** or to produce **activity plans** to support a child or a group of children. It is important to understand the difference between them.

Set of actions

A **set of actions** is used to support development of a child's skills and abilities. Sets of actions are:

- developed to meet the needs of individual children, to support them towards identified goals
- delivered over a period of time and monitored to check progress
- unambiguous and specific, but do not give details of how each action will be carried out (as in an activity plan).

Activity plans

An **activity plan** is a plan for a **specific play and learning activity** that is adult-led or child-initiated. An activity plan:

- sets out specific aims
- shows how the activity will be organised
- gives detailed information about resources and support
- is for a 'one-off' activity to be delivered in one session
- may develop from a set of actions.

Sample response extract

Activity – set of actions

For Timmy, aged 12 months, with communication delay.

1 To gain eye contact when engaging with Timmy during routines (e.g. nappy changing and meal times).

2 To share interactive books on three occasions each day.

In this extract from a **set of actions**, the actions are:
- specific and unambiguous
- appropriate to the age and stage needs of the child
- examples of best practice.

You would be expected to produce a number of actions. You would need to give more than the two actions listed in this extract.

 Links To revise sets of actions, see page 95.

Sample response extract

Activity plan: puppet play

Aims:

- to encourage responses to words
- to respond to simple instructions.

Environment: Sit on a carpeted area away from distractions.

Introduction: Have Timmy sitting opposite and show him a box. Ask 'what's in the box?', encouraging curiosity.

Development: Get out the puppet and use it to communicate – say hello, say the puppet's name, point out interesting things in the room. Watch for Timmy's reaction and use the puppet to respond. Use the puppet to give instructions such as 'give me the car', 'shake my hand'.

In this extract from an **activity plan**, the activity plan is appropriate: to encourage the child to respond to words and instructions.

You should identify the skills and abilities that the child is working towards, when recommending actions or planning activities.

You should devise an activity plan with a structured breakdown of a play session that is likely to support Timmy to acquire the skills expected at his stage of development.

 Links To revise activity plans, see page 96.

Now try this

Look at the set of actions and recommend three more actions to support Timmy's communication skills.

Recommending actions

Here are some examples of skills involved if asked to recommend actions and justify them in response to information given in a case study. If asked to produce a **set of actions** in relation to communication, literacy, numeracy or mathematical development, recommendations must be examples of **good practice** that are **justified** and supported by references to early years **theory**.

> Elina is aged 4 years and attends Crossdale House Nursery.
>
> She is meeting her expected milestones in most areas of the curriculum but a recent assessment shows that her numeracy development is delayed. She attempts to count, but not always in the correct sequence and she cannot recognise numerals.
>
> She lives with her mother and brother, aged 6. Elina's mother has approached the nursery as she has noticed that her numeracy development is slower than her brother's at the same age.

🔗 **Links** The case study follows on from the task brief about Crossdale House Nursery on page 89.

This introduces a child who attends the setting. The case study can give information about a child's stage of development in communication, literacy or numeracy and any developmental delay, additional needs or language needs.

With this example case study, you might be asked to produce a set of actions that can support Elina's development at nursery and at home. You should:

- suggest actions that exemplify best practice
- suggest resources to support actions, including the role of the adult
- justify actions with reference to early years theory.

Factors to consider

To be able to produce a set of actions for Elina, you must first consider:

- ✓ the expected stage of numeracy development of her age
- ✓ what might help Elina to reach the next stage
- ✓ any opportunities during everyday routines and activities
- ✓ available resources
- ✓ how she can be supported by the adult.

Sample response extract

At the age of 4 years Elina would be expected to be able to count to 10 and recognise numerals to 5. The following set of actions show best practice. They can be used in the setting and at home to help Elina to develop her numeracy skills.

1 Use number rhymes with Elina on two occasions each day.
2 Count during everyday routines, such as setting the table.
3 Use small-world play activities for counting practice.
4 Play an object/numeral matching game for 10 minutes each day.
5 Use a computer program for 10 minutes a day for counting along.

Resources: Rhymes, books with pictures, such as 'one, two buckle my shoe', small-world toys for sorting and counting (e.g. farm animals, cars), number games such as dominoes or lotto, computer/number program.

Adult role: Encourage Elina to join in with number rhymes. Engage in Elina's small-world play to encourage sorting, matching and counting, and use open-ended questioning to extend thinking. Join in with number, board and computer games, and model counting and matching numbers. Encourage parents to use opportunities to count with her at home.

In this extract from a response to the case study, the learner has identified the skills and abilities that Elina should be helped towards.

You should identify the learning experiences that will help Elina. You should list them as a set of actions, as these experiences do not have to be broken down in detail as you would in an activity plan.

You should suggest appropriate resources that can support each action.

You need to suggest appropriate strategies that the adult should use to support each of the actions.

Now try this

Add **two** more ideas to the above set of actions for experiences that could support Elina's numeracy.

🔗 **Links** To see how this answer goes on to justify actions with reference to early years theory, look at page 97.

Recommending activity plans

Here are some examples of skills involved if asked to produce activity plans and justify them. For example, you might be asked to design two activities that will support the development of early reading skills for a group of four 3-year-olds at Crossdale House Nursery. The activities must consider the particular needs of one child in the group whose home language is not English.

You would need to produce a plan for each activity, including:

- information about the resources required
- the role of the early years educators and other adults
- how the adults can meet the needs of individual children
- a justification of your activity plans, linking best practice to early years theories.

Links This follows on from the task brief about Crossdale House Nursery on page 89.

Factors to consider

The structure of activity plans should always be the same, but the focus and aims could be different. They must be examples of good practice that are justified and supported by references to early years theory.

You should provide a correct structure for your activity plans:

- ✓ Children in group, names, ages
- ✓ Proposed learning activity goals
- ✓ Description of the activity
- ✓ Environment
- ✓ Resources and equipment
- ✓ Individual or additional needs
- ✓ Role of adult

Sample response extract

Age group: four children aged 3 years.

Learning activity goals: Children will:
- make links between pictures and writing
- develop phonetic awareness.

Activity plan 1: Group story using a big book

Introduction: Ensure that children are comfortable and can see the words and pictures. Show the cover and ask children what they think the story is about.

Development: Read the story, following the words with a finger and pointing out pictures that relate to words. Pause reading before a repetitive part of the story to see if children join in. Draw attention to repeating sounds and words. Point out some rhyming words and see if children can recognise others by describing similarities or patterns.

In this extract from a response, the number of children and age range of the group is given. If only one child is involved, give their name and age.

You should clearly identify the skills or abilities the activity will support, which are appropriate to the age and stage of the children.

You should give a clear description of the activity, describing different stages such as the introduction and activity development.

Now try this

Complete activity plan 1. Use the headings in the structure of the activity plan and:

- identify a suitable environment for the activity
- identify a suitable resource for the activity
- suggest ways in which the adult can support a child whose home language is not English.

This activity is adult-led, so the adult's role is included in the activity description. In child-initiated activities, you may need to write a separate section on how adults can engage with children as they play.

Links To see how this answer goes on to justify actions with reference to early years theory, see page 97.

Relating to theories

Here are some examples of skills involved when justifying your recommendations, showing how you have taken into consideration **best practice** by making references to relevant early years **theories**.

Making links to best practice

These are theories you need to consider when making links to best practice.

- **Bruner:** Language Acquisition Support System (LASS), scaffolding, three modes of representation
- **Vygotsky:** social constructivist theory, Zone of Proximal Development (ZPD)
- **Roger Brown:** five stages of speech and language development
- **Piaget:** constructivist theory, stages of development – sensorimotor and pre-operational stages of learning
- **Chomsky:** Language Acquisition Device (LAD)

 Links Look at pages 53–56 to revise how these theories can help to explain best practice.

Sample response extract

Constructivists such as Piaget, Vygotsky and Bruner believed that children develop their cognitive ability through experiences in their environment. Therefore, using everyday routines and giving opportunities to learn through play is good practice. According to Piaget, children will construct meaning and develop schemas through hands-on activity. A criticism of Piaget is that he did not recognise the importance of the adult in supporting children to progress, believing that children must reach a stage of 'readiness' for that to happen. Vygotsky and Bruner found that with adult support children could reach the next stage. Vygotsky referred to the level of understanding that children reach with help as the 'Zone of Proximal Development' and Bruner described the process of 'scaffolding'. This helps to explain how modelling counting and supporting Elina to count herself is likely to be effective in promoting her progress.

 Links This is an extract from a justification for the set of actions on page 95.

You should refer to three theorists who have contributed to our understanding of cognitive development. It is important to use at least two theories to support your recommendations.

You should use correct terminology relating to these theories – it can be helpful to include such terms in your notes.

Sample response extract

It is good practice for children to have the opportunity to interact with books in a variety of ways, rather than just reading a story. This helps them to 'construct' their own meaning, which is at the foundation of constructivist theories of learning.

According to Bruner's modes of representation, at the age of 4 years children are in the iconic mode. This helps to explain how children are thinking and learning. As children start to think symbolically, they will begin to develop an understanding that the symbols (words and sentences) in a book carry meaning. Using pictures alongside words is important at this age and stage to help them to develop links between words and pictures and their phonemic awareness.

 Links This is an extract from a justification for the activity plan on page 96.

This extract links theories to good practice, showing an understanding that it is important for children to 'construct' their own understanding through activities.

You should show that you understand stages and learning modes from the theories and the importance of this for effective planning.

Now try this

Write **two** or more sentences to justify your planned activity referring to Vygotsky's ZPD theory.

Purpose of research

The aim of a particular piece of research is usually to answer a specific question, to find out information or gain knowledge.

Research in early years

There are four **key purposes** of research in early years.

1 To improve **outcomes** for children and their families

2 To inform **policy and practice**

3 To extend **knowledge and understanding**

4 To identify **gaps in provision**

Research leading to improvement

Research in the early years sector explores different issues such as improving children's diet, caring for vulnerable children or identifying the importance of play.

Research helps to form policy that leads to improvements in early years practice.

What is research?

Research is a systematic or orderly procedure that explores issues to establish facts or reach new conclusions.

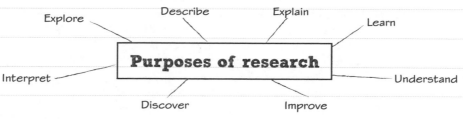

Explore   Describe   Explain   Learn

Purposes of research

Interpret   Understand

Discover   Improve

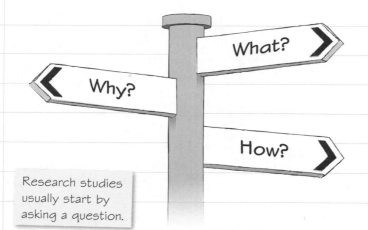

Why?   What?   How?

Research studies usually start by asking a question.

Questions that lead to research

Here are three examples of types of questions that led to important research projects.

1 **What** is the cost of childcare in different types of early years settings?

2 **Why** do some families have difficulty accessing children's services and others do not?

3 **How** can children be encouraged to make healthy food choices?

Now try this

Make up a question of your own that could start a research study, using 'What', 'Why' or 'How'. Show how your question relates to the purposes of research in the early years sector.

The four purposes of research in the early years sector are covered on this page. Your question should relate to one or more of these purposes.

Issues in early years practice

Issues of concern in early years practice focus on legislation and types of service that assess and meet children's needs.

Research leads to improvements in early years provision, policy and practice. Sometimes reviews are conducted as a reaction to a particular event, such as the death of a child. Such reviews can be forms of research.

Types of issues

The three main types of issues for research in the early years sector are:

1 early years provision and how services work together

2 early years pedagogy

3 the principles and themes of the Early Years Foundation Stage.

What to research

When planning research, you can look at what is 'topical' by reading early years journals, following the news or organisations in your field.

Provision

Research into early years provision could look at:

- the effectiveness of different types of provision
- the effects of the introduction of free early years provision
- how the principles of the early years curriculum are interpreted in practice
- the benefits of multi-agency working
- how services recognise and meet the needs of children who are disadvantaged or with additional needs.

Pedagogy

Research into methods used for teaching and learning could look at:

- how early years practitioners support learning
- how children learn from each other
- how children develop biologically and socially.

Links See page 100 to revise more on the Early Years Foundation Stage curriculum (EYFS).

Here are a few examples of recent research and research that is currently under way.

- 'The Common Assessment Framework from 9 years on: a creative process'
- 'Creating more participatory practice for children in early years: an action research project'
- 'How do practitioners create inclusive environments in day care settings for children under the age of five years with chronic health conditions? An exploratory case study'
- 'Young childrens and families' experiences of services aimed at reducing the impact of low-income: Participation work with children and families'
- 'Reception baseline comparability study'

Now try this

A major current challenge facing the early years sector is how early years services work together to recognise children at risk of abuse. Suggest a related research topic for each of the three types of issues identified on this page. Find out how research in these areas has influenced policy or practice.

 Watch the news, read a newspaper or search the internet for current ideas.

Issues and the EYFS

The **Early Years Foundation Stage** (EYFS) is a statutory document, introduced in 2008 to improve the outcomes for children from birth up to 5 years. All Ofsted-registered early years providers must adhere to the requirements of the EYFS. Issues around the EYFS may focus on its success in improving children's outcomes.

Types of issue

Research may be in relation to requirements for:

- learning and development
- assessment
- aims and principles of the EYFS
- safeguarding and welfare.

Individuals involved

Research may involve:

- children and how they respond to the curriculum
- practitioners and their experiences in delivering the EYFS
- parents/carers and their views on provision.

EYFS research

There are many research opportunities relating to the EYFS. Here are some suggestions in four key areas.

1 **Learning and development requirements**

- The balance between child-initiated and adult-led play
- The effectiveness of assessment at the age of 2 and 5 years
- The provision of outdoor space for learning

2 **Aims and objectives**

- The benefits of partnership working between practitioners and parents
- What makes children 'school ready'
- The consistency of provision across different settings

3 **Principles**

- The effectiveness of the key person role
- The features of an enabling environment
- How the curriculum takes into account each child's individual needs

4 **Safeguarding and welfare**

- Health and safety practice
- Encouraging healthy food choices
- Approaches to managing behaviour

Children in early years settings must feel safe and included, and be able to access the curriculum.

Now try this

Recognising that each child is unique is an important EYFS principle. This means that early years settings are required to ensure that every child is able to access the curriculum, feel safe and included. Suggest **two** different research topics concerning the principle of inclusion.

Planning research

It is important to plan each piece of research carefully with an understanding of the research methodologies, ethical issues, and planning and research skills involved.

The research process

Key stages of the research process include:

1 research planning, rationale and objectives (pages 101–102)

2 using research methodology (pages 103–106)

3 selecting target group and sample (page 107)

4 considering ethical issues (pages 108–113)

5 conducting research and selecting, analysing and interpreting sources (pages 114–122) and evaluation and application of research (pages 123–134).

Achievable objectives

Research objectives should be SMART.

- **S**pecific
- **M**easurable
- **A**chievable
- **R**ealistic
- **T**ime-related

Project proposal

Developing a project proposal helps identify and structure the detailed steps of a study. A project proposal outline may include:

- rationale, achievable objectives, measures for success
- research question/hypothesis
- research design. What form will the research take? What methods will it use? Who is the target group and sample?
- ethical issues, including considerations for consent and for preventing harm
- when and how the research will be conducted. How will interpretation of the data take place? How will it be monitored and modified if need be?
- when and how the evaluation of research will take place. How will conclusions be drawn and presented? What are the implications for future research, practice and provision?

Timescales and monitoring

Researchers often use calendars or charts to plan timescales and produce a visual project plan. They break down the stages to a timeline and create a tick list to monitor progress. This helps to check the progress and quality of research on a weekly basis and reflect on progress regularly. If something isn't working, it can be changed so it is back on track.

Select research methods

Research methods need to show reliability of results. **Triangulation** uses different research methods to investigate the same research question from different angles and increases the validity of the results. For example:

☑ **observations**: tracker observations to see behaviours of children

☑ **structured interviews**: with the child's parents, to find out about their views

☑ **questionnaires**: to practitioners asking them for their views on play provision for children.

Now try this

1 What does 'triangulation' mean?

2 What is the benefit of triangulation?

3 State **three** things to consider when setting and monitoring realistic timescales.

Rationale for research

When planning a piece of research, it is important to identify the **topic** and **rationale** (the reason for doing the research).

Choosing a research topic

Choose a topic that will:

- draw on a personal interest
- sustain your interest for the whole project
- be relevant to your work
- be achievable
- be ethical.

Breadth of topic

Start with a broad topic area and then narrow down your focus. Here is an example.

> **Field:** Education

↓

> **Issue:** Discrimination in education

↓

> **Narrow issue:** Are special schools more able to meet the needs of children with physical disability than mainstream schools?

Case study

 Topic

For 5 years, Gill has been working with an organisation carrying out key research into children in social care. Some of the children have experienced multiple foster carers. The organisation is aware that this affects the children's behaviour, and Gill is interested in exploring the impact it has on their confidence and self-esteem. So Gill has focused in on her field (children in care) and broad topic (the impact on children of having multiple foster carers).

 Rationale

The charity's rationale (or reason) for doing the research is the view that frequent changes of foster parents are detrimental to children's well-being. By doing research, Gill may be able to gather evidence to support this **hypothesis**. This could lead to a change in the way children in care are managed.

Hypothesis
This is an idea or possible explanation for something, based on limited evidence, which is used as a starting point for an investigation.

 Research title

Gill has to decide on a working title for her research. A title should give an idea of what the study is about. So Gill's research title could be:

'Exploring the impact of being placed with multiple foster parents on children's psychological well-being'.

④ **Research questions**

Gill has decided to investigate these specific research questions.

- What is the impact on children's psychological well-being when experiencing frequent changes in foster parents?
- Does the impact differ with children's gender and age?

Now try this

Choose one of these research issues.

1 Outdoor play
2 Take up of free places for 2-year-olds
3 Children whose home language is not English

Then: (a) narrow down your research to a detailed issue; (b) suggest a rationale for researching the issue; (c) decide on a working title.

To help you complete this activity, follow the steps in the 'breadth of topic' box and then the same process as Gill in the case study above.

Quantitative methods

Quantitative research produces data that can be analysed statistically (e.g. the number of hours spent playing outdoors). The data are measurable and can be used to generate a hypothesis (e.g. 'children who do not play outdoors are at higher risk of infection').

Controlled conditions

Quantitative research looks **objectively** at attitudes, opinions, responses and other aspects of human behaviour to learn about the way children behave and act in their everyday lives. Quantitative research is usually used to explore an issue using controlled situations. This means that the level of control and observation is high, limiting the variables.

Piaget used observational experiments to study the age that children develop logical thought. For example, prior to logical thought, a child might say the tall jar contains most liquid although they have observed identical quantities poured into both glasses.

Experiments

Quantitative research looks at the effects of one thing on another (cause and effect) using **experiments**. For example, if you want to find out whether boys choose 'boy toys', such as trucks, and girls choose 'girl toys', such as dolls, you could set out toys and then individually invite girls and boys to make a choice and watch the reaction of each child.

In this experiment the **hypothesis** would be: 'If you give children a choice they will always choose "gender-specific toys".'

Producing quantitative data

Numerical data for **quantitative analysis** can be produced using six key methods.

① Experiments   ③ Interviews   ⑤ Questionnaires

② Observations   ④ Checklists   ⑥ Surveys

Using closed questions

Quantitative questionnaires and surveys usually contain 'closed questions' that require only a yes or no answer. For example, it is possible to establish:

 how many children are in a category (e.g. attend a nursery)

 frequency (e.g. number of hours that each child attends the nursery each week)

 specialised information (e.g. number of children whose home language is not English).

Analysing quantitative data

Quantitative experiments are usually analysed numerically and by making **statistical inferences**. This means that conclusions can be drawn based on what the data indicate. An example is data compiled from local authorities and GP surgeries to identify whether methods of care and support, or treatment for children's health conditions, are successful, and to identify trends.

Presenting quantitative data

Some key ways of presenting quantitative data are using a histogram, bar chart, a line graph, a pie chart, or charts that show the mean, the mode and the median.

 Links Look at pages 125–127 to revise interpretation of quantitative data.

Now try this

What data are produced by quantitative research?

Qualitative methods

Qualitative research produces data that are descriptive and cannot easily be measured statistically (e.g. emotions shown by facial expression). Research takes place through words about how the child feels (e.g. their worries on their first day in the reception class).

Listening to people

Qualitative methods are used to look **subjectively** at human behaviour and to interpret what participants say about how they feel and experience things.

Qualitative research is commonly used in the early years as it is the best way to understand what children say and to observe what they do.

Qualitative research may be used alongside quantitative research. For example, finding the number of children choosing a particular play activity (quantitative) and then exploring the reasons for their choice (qualitative).

Qualitative research is sometimes called **exploratory** because it explores reasons and motivations for children or other relevant people saying and doing things.

Producing qualitative data

In qualitative research you try to develop understanding of what the child, parent or carer says by analysing their words and actions. The researcher may ask participants to provide explanations of their feelings, opinions and experiences. Or they may observe behaviour and interpret what behaviours may suggest.

Using open questions

Qualitative research methods, such as interviews, usually contain 'open questions' that require an answer with a description or explanation, e.g. 'Why did you choose this nursery for your child?'

1 **Diary studies** – a diary is kept and analysed by researchers. This usually takes place over a long period of time.

2 **Case study** – an up-close, in-depth examination of a subject.

3 **Focus group** – where groups of children, parents or practitioners are asked about their opinions, attitudes and experiences.

7 **Vignette notes** – the use of hypothetical stories based on real situations that can be used to support in-depth interviews or group discussion.

Key methods of qualitative research

4 **Questionnaires** – using open questions.

6 **Observations** – of children's behaviours in different situations.

5 **Interviews** – asking focused questions about opinions, attitudes or experiences.

Now try this

1 What are qualitative methods usually used to explore?

2 Give **two** examples of a method you could use in qualitative research.

You need to be able to:
• choose and evaluate appropriate research methods
• identify and evaluate methods in research carried out by others.

 Links Look at pages 128–130 to revise interpretation of qualitative data.

Advantages and disadvantages

You must be aware of the suitability of methods in order to make decisions on the validity and reliability of results.

 Observations

Observations can produce both **qualitative** and **quantitative** data. The observer may look on (as a non-participant) or observe as they take part in the activity (as a participant).

Advantages	Disadvantages
Observer can see what is happening	Participants may be uncomfortable
Not expensive to carry out	People may behave differently when being watched
Data can be more reliable	Time-consuming

 Experiments

Experimentation usually produces **quantitative** data.

Advantages	Disadvantages
Good for discovering cause and effect	Not typical of real-life situations
Allows control over variables	Behaviour of participants may be limited
Can be replicated	Participants may guess purpose of research and subconsciously influence the data

Covert and overt observation

In **covert observations** the participants are not made aware that they are being observed, while in **overt observations** the participants are aware of being observed and the reasons for the observation.

 Interviews

Interviews can be used to gather both **qualitative** and **quantitative** data.

Advantages	Disadvantages
Direct feedback from participants	Time-consuming and costly
Topics can be explored in depth	Researchers need to be well prepared
Opportunities to explain and clarify	Researcher may be influenced by their own opinion, biasing the results

 Questionnaires and surveys

Questionnaires and surveys can produce **qualitative** or **quantitative** data.

Advantages	Disadvantages
Can gain large amounts of information	Doesn't always give insight into feelings, motivations or behaviours
Can be carried out quickly	Participant may not tell the truth
Cheap and not time-consuming	Questions may be misinterpreted

Using qualitative and quantitative methods

When qualitative and quantitative methods are used together, it can be known as **mixed methods** design.

Advantages	Disadvantages
In-depth information	Time-consuming
Increases reliability	Difficult to manage
Increases validity	Can be difficult to analyse

Q1 What colour do you like best?

Red ☐   Green ☐   Orange ☐

Q2 What is it about this colour that you like best?

_____

This research uses a mixed method design. It is possible to find out **how many** children like red jelly beans but also **why** they like red jelly beans.

Now try this

1 Describe a research method you could use to find out the benefits of the key person approach for the child and their parent.

2 Give **one** advantage and **one** disadvantage of using this method.

 State your method and explain briefly how you could carry out the research.

105

Research questions

When planning and conducting research, you need to think carefully about the types of questions you ask in order to achieve the reliable results that you need.

Research questions

Here are some examples of research questions for qualitative studies.

Question 1:

What do children think of good behaviour rewards used in Year 1?

Sub-question:

What are the effects of using good behaviour rewards for children in Year 1?

Question 2:

What are the effects of poverty on children's outcomes?

Sub-question:

Does free education for 2-year-olds who are in poverty affect their outcomes?

Closed and open questions

Closed and open questions can be used in interviews, questionnaires and surveys.

Here's an example of a **closed question**.

* Which type of early years setting did you choose for your child?

Here's an example of an **open question**.

* Tell me, why did you choose this particular type of setting for your child?

Questionnaires can be completed on paper or onscreen.

Scaled questions

Some questions ask respondents to select their answer from a scale, such as from strongly disagree to strongly agree, or to rate their response according to a number scale, perhaps from 1 to 10. These scales are sometimes referred to as **Likert** scales. These questions allow a wider variety of responses than closed questions but answers can still be analysed systematically. Here is an example.

I am satisfied with the play provision at my child's nursery.

Agree strongly ☐   Agree ☐   Neither agree nor disagree ☐   Disagree ☐   Disagree strongly ☐

Now try this

Which of these questions are open and which are closed?

(a) Is your child attending a nursery?

(b) Have you ever visited other nurseries?

(c) How do you think outdoor play affects children?

(d) Why do you think it is good for children to start looking at books early in life?

(e) How much time do you spend reading with your child on average each day?

(f) At what age did your child start to walk?

Target groups and samples

The **target group** or **target population** is the subset of the whole population that is relevant to your research. When planning, conducting, reporting and evaluating research you need to be able to identify the target population for a particular research project.

A sample is a subset of the target group included in your research. The challenge is to ensure that the sample is **representative** of the target group.

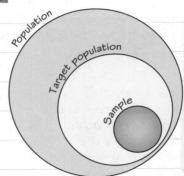

If you wanted to research attitudes to services for children and families your target population might be adults in the UK with children between birth and 5 years. Your sample should be selected to represent the target population as accurately as possible.

Sampling methods

Researchers cannot gather data from every member of the target group. Instead they select a **sample** from the target population. Researchers then use data from the sample to make **predictions** about the whole target population. Here are **four** different types of sampling you need to know about.

Advantages of sampling

 It is **cheaper** to gather data from a sample than a whole target population.

 It is **quicker** to collect data from a sample.

 It is **easier** to analyse data from a sample and calculate statistics.

1 Random sample

Every member of the target group has an equal chance of being chosen.

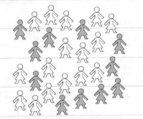

Picking names out of a hat would produce a random sample.

3 Stratified random sample

The target group is divided into subsets (called **strata**). A proportional number of members of each stratum is randomly selected for the sample.

There are twice as many boys as girls, so twice as many boys are included in the sample.

2 Systematic sampling (*k*-in-1 sample)

Every *k*th member of the target group is selected for the sample.

Choosing every fifth member of the target population would produce a k-in-1 sample.

4 Cluster sample

The target group is divided into subsets. One or more entire subset is selected for the sample.

The target group has been divided into boys and girls. All the girls have been selected for this cluster sample.

Case study

For Gill's research (outlined on page 102), she has chosen a stratified random sampling procedure. She will divide her target group of children into two age groups and randomly select three girls and three boys from each of the two groups.

Now try this

A primary school wants to research the diet of its learners.

1 Identify the target population for this research.

2 Describe **two** different sampling methods the school could use for this research.

Describe your sampling methods as specifically as possible.

Ethical principles

When planning, conducting, reporting and evaluating research, researchers must be ethical. This includes showing respect for the participants and treating them according to some basic principles.

Being ethical

Being ethical means that you conduct yourself according to certain standards, and treat children and others properly. A **code of conduct** may be used to spell out the standards of behaviour that are required.

Research involving children

The International Charter for Ethical Research Involving Children (ERIC) sets out seven commitments that work to maintain the status, rights and well-being of children. 'Respecting the dignity of children' is a main concern of the organisation.

Some ethical principles

Ethics are guidelines. Here are some ethical principles that could guide any aspect of human behaviour, from how we conduct ourselves in our personal lives, to behaviour in business and research.

- Promote the truth.
- Avoid error.
- Cooperate and collaborate.
- Maintain confidentiality.
- Be accountable.
- Be trustworthy.
- Be professional.
- Respect the dignity of participants.
- Respect **human rights**.

All research should be **ethical**, must be carried out according to a strict code of conduct and should not cause harm to consenting participants. In the case of subjects under 18, both the parent and, where possible, the child, are required to give their consent, which may be withdrawn at any time.

Ethics in research

The following are examples of organisations that conduct research projects and have a set of principles for ethical conduct in those research activities.

- British Educational Research Association (BERA)
- National Children's Bureau (NCB)
- Centre for Research in Early Childhood (CREC)
- National Society for the Prevention of Cruelty to Children (NSPCC).

Universities and other centres of research usually have an **ethics committee** to oversee research projects.

Nuremberg Code

This set of ethical principles guides research on human subjects and was devised in 1947 following the Nuremberg Trials at the end of the Second World War.

Researchers, harm and consent

Researchers have a duty not to cause harm to their subjects through their research. Harm could be **physical**, **emotional** or **material** (to property).

In order to avoid causing harm, researchers should behave ethically, following appropriate codes of conduct, and must gain **informed consent** from participants. Participants must understand what is going to happen during the research and formally agree to take part. The principle of consent is central to the Nuremberg Code. **Mental capacity** is required in order to give informed consent.

 Look at page 111 to revise informed consent.

Now try this

1 Name **three** ethical principles.
2 What is the main purpose of an ethical code of conduct?

Safeguarding ethics

When planning, conducting, reporting and evaluating research, researchers must ensure that no harm is caused to participants or wider society. Correct conduct in research has implications for the whole of society.

Risk assessment

Researchers have a duty to minimise exposure to risk when children, parents or others take part in research. Risk assessment is used to identify and mitigate sources of possible harm.

Identify potential risk → Assess risk to participant → Identify ways to control risk → Evaluate controls → (back to Identify potential risk)

Data protection

Researchers must follow the law (Data Protection Act 1998) and their organisation's **data protection policy and procedures** when they keep data and documents about participants or use photographs. This helps to ensure appropriate use of data and participant **confidentiality**.

- Personal data should be stored in a locked cabinet or on a password-protected computer.
- When you report data you should not use actual names or refer to traceable locations.
- Data can only be used for the purpose for which it was collected and for which the data provider gave their consent.

 Links   Look at page 112 to revise the Data Protection Act 1998.

Conflicts of interest

Conflicts of interest in research should be avoided by:

- **peer review** (scrutiny of research findings by another expert in the field prior to publication)
- **participant review**, whereby a child or their parent, carer or others who took part in the research are given the opportunity to comment and may ask that their data are excluded
- **mentoring** by an expert, allowing researchers to discuss their work with another professional
- maintaining a **professional distance** so that objectivity is ensured
- protection of people who **disclose** ethical concerns through **whistle-blowing procedures**.

Impact of unethical conduct through misuse of results

The case of Andrew Wakefield is a good example of how misconduct in research impacts on society. Wakefield was the author of a *Lancet* paper that linked autism with the MMR (measles, mumps, rubella) vaccine. Following a 2-year investigation, Wakefield was found guilty of conflict of interest, selective reporting of data and unethical dealings with children.

Wakefield's paper resulted in a fall in the take-up of the MMR vaccine and an increase in the incidence of these preventable diseases, which can have dangerous side effects.

Now try this

1. Identify **one** key procedure researchers should follow under the Data Protection Act 1998 to ensure participant confidentiality.
2. Name **two** ways of preventing conflict of interest in research.

Confidentiality

When planning and conducting research, participants must know that their information remains **confidential**. Researchers have a **professional duty** to make sure that confidentiality is **safeguarded**.

Why is confidentiality important?

Successful research relies on participants volunteering truthful **personal information** about their health, feelings, beliefs, attitudes and actions.

They are more likely to provide honest responses when they **trust** the researcher not to divulge their information.

What is professionalism?

Professionalism means having the qualities, skills, competence and behaviours expected of individuals belonging to your profession.

Safeguarding confidentiality is an aspect of professionalism in research.

Confidentiality for all participants

Depending on the focus of research, early years practitioners and other professionals may be considered as participants. Researchers have a duty to protect the confidentiality of participants, whatever their role.

Participants' names

Locations of organisations and settings

Confidential information

Other identifying features of participants, organisations and settings

Names of organisations and settings

Gatekeepers

Researchers sometimes need to gain **gatekeeper approval** for research. The gatekeeper is the person responsible for allowing research to take place in their setting. Issues of confidentiality would focus on the gatekeeper's identity and the name and location of the setting.

If you are observing daily routines in an early years setting, you will need to gain gatekeeper approval.

How is confidentiality protected?

Confidentiality is protected through:

- the law, e.g. Data Protection Act 1998
- organisational data protection policies and procedures that implement the 1998 Act
- Freedom of Information Act 2000
- a professional approach
- professional codes of conduct
- ethical research codes, such as the International Charter for Ethical Research Involving Children (ERIC)
- regulatory bodies (see page 108 for organisations that regulate ethics in research)
- anonymising data.

Anonymity

Research data that has been **anonymised** cannot be traced back to the original providers of the data, although pieces of data from each individual are linked together for analysis. When referring to children, other participants or settings, researchers can use initials or reference numbers instead of names.

Now try this

1 What information should always remain confidential in research studies involving individual human participants?

2 What information should always remain confidential in research studies involving observations of large groups?

Be aware of the different information that should be protected in various types of research study.

Informed consent

When planning and conducting research, you must always obtain a participant's or, for young children their parent or carer's, consent before proceeding with the research. Informed consent is an important principle of the Nuremberg Code and is central to professional conduct in research. Understanding and agreement together make up informed consent.

① Understanding

It is important that the child's parent or other participants are fully aware of what they are being asked to do and assess whether they wish to take any risks that may be associated with the research. To be **informed**, the child's parent or other participants must understand:

- the aims of the research
- potential benefits to policy, practice and provision procedure
- what will happen during the research project
- any potential risks in taking part
- how their data will be treated
- what will happen to the results at the end.

The child, their parent, or other participants must also have the opportunity to ask questions about the project and to have their concerns addressed.

② Agreement

In giving their consent, the participant agrees to take part in the study that the researcher has described (or to allow their child to take part). If the project changes in any way, further informed consent is required.

Obtaining informed consent

Remember that participants may include early years practitioners and other early years professionals, as well as children. All participants must give informed consent.

Capacity

In order to give informed consent, the child's parent or carer must be able to understand the project and agree to take part. They must have a certain level of mental capacity to achieve this. Children may also give their consent to take part in research if they are able to, but a parent or carer must also give their informed consent.

Vulnerable groups

Special safeguards should be in place when undertaking research involving vulnerable individuals. Vulnerable groups include:

- children aged under 16
- the elderly
- those lacking mental capacity
- parents or carers lacking capacity
- parents or carers with learning or communication difficulties.

Safeguarding children

Children should be protected in research and be accompanied by a parent or responsible adult when being interviewed or observed. This ensures they are treated properly, their human rights are protected and the information they give is recorded without bias.

A responsible person, such as a parent or carer, must give consent for a child to take part in research.

Now try this

1 What does 'informed consent' mean?
2 Why is it important to gain informed consent from all participants?
3 Why should you take account of the participant's level of understanding when asking for consent?

Legislation

When planning, conducting, reporting and evaluating research, researchers have to adhere to a number of different legislative frameworks. You need to know about legislation that is current at the time of delivery of the research and applicable to England, Wales or Northern Ireland, including the Data Protection Act 1998 and the Human Rights Act 1998.

The Data Protection Act 1998

The Data Protection Act (DPA) 1998 is an Act of Parliament covering the UK and Northern Ireland. It sets out the law on how to **collect, store and process the personal data** of individuals living in the UK, including those who have taken part in research.

Principles of the DPA 1998

Personal information must be:

1. used fairly and lawfully
2. used for specified and limited purposes
3. adequate, relevant and not excessive
4. accurate and up to date
5. kept for no longer than necessary
6. processed under the terms of the Act
7. kept securely
8. not transferred to a country outside the EU.

How to store data

- Computers and other electronic devices should be password protected.
- Physical documents should be stored in a locked filing cabinet.

Researchers need specific consent to take and store **photographs** and **video** footage of research participants.

Timescale

Researchers need consent to store and reuse participants' data. The DPA 1998 does not define how long data can be stored. When deciding what is an acceptable timescale, researchers should consider how they might use data, for example:

- for further research into the subject
- to write an article or book at a later date.

The Human Rights Act 1998

There are aspects of the Human Rights Act 1998 that researchers should adhere to when conducting research. You do not need to have an in-depth knowledge of the Act, but it is important to know how the Articles of the Act relate to research, including:

- **Article 3:** No person should be subjected to torture and inhuman or degrading treatment.
- **Article 8:** All individuals have the right to respect of their private and family life, home and correspondence.
- **Article 9:** All individuals have the right to freedom of thought, conscience and religion.

United Nations Convention on the Rights of the Child (UNCRC)

Developed in 1989, the **UNCRC** drew up an international legally binding agreement on the rights of children. Articles that are relevant in research are as follows.

- **Article 2:** Children must not be discriminated against, whatever their background, status or ability.
- **Article 3:** The best interests of children should be the primary concern.
- **Article 12:** Children's views and opinions must be respected.
- **Article 34:** Children must be protected from sexual exploitation.

Now try this

1. Give **two** principles of the Data Protection Act 1998.
2. Identify **one** Article from the Human Rights Act 1998 that relates to research participants.
3. How does the UNCRC safeguard children in research?

 Safeguarding of confidentiality is the common theme in these Acts. Other rights are protected too.

 Links See pages 108–111 to revise ethical principles and confidentiality.

Non-judgemental practice

When planning, conducting, reporting and evaluating research, researchers must remain objective so that the research is unbiased.

Are you judgemental?

☑ Do you have strong opinions about things or are you able to keep an open mind?

☑ Are you good at separating facts from opinions?

Being **non-judgemental** and **objective** are important skills in research.

Whether providing education or conducting research in the early years sector, rejecting stereotypes, prejudice and discrimination is important.

Rejecting bias

Taking an objective standpoint is vital to good research. It means you don't pre-empt the outcomes of your research and you keep an open mind about the possible results. To be objective, you must be aware of and reject stereotypes, prejudice and discrimination.

- A **stereotype** is a set idea about a group of people that does not reflect their individuality.
- **Prejudice** is an unjustified attitude based on an individual's membership of a particular group. Prejudice is often connected to stereotyping.
- **Discrimination** is the unfair treatment of a person owing to prejudice.

Bias is usually unintentional, so it can be difficult to counter. Bias leads to a decrease in the validity of results and even to outright errors.

Researcher bias

If you are **biased**, it means you have already made up your mind about something. If you approach research with a bias (an expectation of a particular outcome), you can influence your findings. For example, you can change how children, parents or others respond to you by the questions that you ask and by the way that you ask them. In addition, you may interpret results to give you the answer you expect!

Consider these two questions.

- How do you feel about cuts in children's centre provision? (open question)
- Do you think cuts in children's centre provision are terrible? (leading question)

Sample bias

This is bias in the way the sample is selected.

If you only contact people who have complained about an early years setting to ask them about their level of satisfaction, you will not get an accurate picture of how the setting is performing.

Bias in data collection

If you are unaware of the potential for bias, you might only log data that support your hypothesis as these will be more obvious to you.

Objectivity and subjectivity

Objectivity	Subjectivity
Fact	Opinion
What actually happened	An attitude or judgement
Can be proved true or false	Cannot be proved true or false

Now try this

1. Why is it important to take an objective approach to your research?
2. What is bias and how can it arise?

Primary and secondary research

When planning, carrying out, reporting and evaluating research, you need to be aware of the two types of research, and their selection for suitability and reliability: **primary** and **secondary**.

Primary research

Primary research (also known as **field research**) involves gathering information (data) that has not been collected before.

Primary research methods include:

- observations
- interviews and focus groups
- case studies
- questionnaires and surveys
- scientific experiments.

Secondary research

Secondary research is sometimes known as **desk-based research** and involves gathering together and analysing existing data. **Sources for secondary research** include:

- professional journals
- professional bodies
- articles
- textbooks
- periodicals
- research organisation websites.

Advantages and disadvantages

The purpose of **primary research** is usually to answer a specific question or to test a hypothesis in an **original** way.

- 👍 The only way to answer a new question
- 👍 Ownership of the research
- 👍 Interactive
- 👍 Meet lots of different people
- 👍 Can control exactly what information you want to collect
- 👍 Can control the reliability of the data
- 👍 More varied work
- 👍 Current
- 👎 Expensive and time-consuming
- 👎 Best carried out by suitably qualified professionals
- 👎 Need to be careful not to let own opinion or expectation affect conclusions drawn

Advantages and disadvantages

Secondary research, such as a literature search, is useful to find out more about a topic in preparation for a piece of primary research. It can also be used to bring together the findings of several different pieces of primary research, which provide better proof of a theory when taken together.

- 👍 Good way to research the background of a topic
- 👍 Quick and inexpensive
- 👍 Can draw together evidence from disparate sources
- 👍 Useful as back-up data when testing a theory using primary research
- 👍 May have the benefit of drawing from a range of primary sources
- 👎 Sources not always reliable
- 👎 Findings may have been biased or unethically gathered
- 👎 Sample size may be too small or target group may influence the findings
- 👎 Information may not exist
- 👎 Less current as conducted at a previous point in time
- 👎 Danger of picking only those sources that support your idea

Now try this

1 What is the difference between primary and secondary research?
2 Give **two** examples of primary research methods and two of secondary research methods.

Primary and secondary research are complementary strategies and serve different purposes.

Literature review

When undertaking research, and in your assessment task for this unit, you need the skills to conduct a literature review of an issue and to know about different types of sources.

What is a literature review?

A literature review is sometimes called a **literature search**. It involves:

- reading and reviewing a wide range of literature regarding a particular issue, to gain a deeper understanding and find out what has been researched before to inform your own research question
- knowledge about primary and secondary sources
- evaluating how reliable a source is – to do this you need to understand where researchers have gathered their information from.

Sources

Primary sources are original documents or eye-witness accounts. Examples are original accounts, letters, diaries, memoirs, official records, photographs and reports that are written soon after the event.

Secondary sources are second-hand accounts based on a review of one or more primary sources. They may offer different perspectives, analysis and conclusions, based on examination of multiple primary sources.

Telling the difference

How do researchers **distinguish** between primary and secondary sources?

Consider: How does the author know the information?

> ✅ Were they present at the event they are recording?
>
> ✅ Does the information come from personal experience?
>
> For example, **Piaget talking about his work** is a **primary source**.

OR

> ✅ Is the author reporting on historical events or on material that is written by others?
>
> ✅ Are conclusions based on many pieces of evidence?
>
> For example, **an author discussing Piaget's work** is a **secondary source**.

Secondary sources versus secondary research

Don't confuse secondary sources with secondary research.

✅ A literature review is an example of **secondary research** – it may examine both primary and secondary research. It uses mostly secondary sources.

✅ A **secondary source** is an interpretation of a primary source.

Your set task

In your set task for this unit you will be provided with a research article and asked to research **at least two secondary sources** related to the issue. In the context of your set task this means you will undertake a literature review for research that relates to the issue in the article you are given. References to secondary sources in this context refer to literature that **you** find to use in your set task.

🔗 **Links** The advantages and disadvantages of primary and secondary sources are the same as those of primary and secondary research, which can be revised on page 114.

Now try this

1 What is the difference between secondary research and secondary sources?
2 What is the purpose of a literature review?
3 Give **one** example of a primary source and **one** example of a secondary source of information.

Notes and records of sources

It is important to make **notes** and to **record** and **organise** the information that you find out during your **literature review**. This is when you research with sources related to your issue and find out about research in related areas. Good organisational skills will make you work more efficiently and improve your time management skills.

Organising your notes

When you carry out your literature searches, you need to make sure you organise your notes so you can find information again. You will need to refer to this information later, as you work with and write up your final report.

There are many ways that you can organise your research.

- ✓ Computerised records
- ✓ Keep a diary
- ✓ Sticky notes
- ✓ Index cards

Effective systems

- **Computerised records**, such as spreadsheets, are easy to keep, update and search.
  - Record your information systematically by being careful to complete every field in a spreadsheet.
  - Remember to back up important data.
- An **index card system** is an effective way of recording information on key findings of relevant literature.
  - A disadvantage can be the need to remember the name and content of each study when searching to find it.

What to record

You need to be able to recall the key features of any piece of literature. To enable you to do this, you should include:

- title
- author
- source and publisher (e.g. journal, government site)
- date of publication
- page numbers, (e.g. journal pages, if applicable)
- if web page, date accessed
- URL
- key points: e.g. what the research was about, methods (such as observations and interviews), key findings
- connections with other sources of information.

Research cycle

The focus of your research may change as you find out more information during your literature review, so it is important to **monitor** and **modify** as you go along.

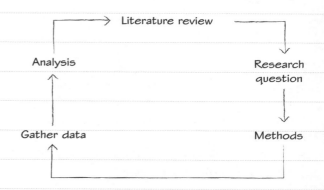

Now try this

Research one piece of literature of your choosing on the advantages and disadvantages of starting nursery at the age of 3. Note and organise a record of your research using a spreadsheet or index card.

 Refer to the list on this page of what to record to make sure that you note all the relevant information.

Reading techniques

Different aspects of your research require different reading techniques for different purposes. You might read in **four** different ways.

 ## Skim reading

Skim reading means you:

- run your eyes over the text
- read material rapidly
- take in basic information
- get the gist of what it's about.

People sometimes skim a newspaper for general news or a travel brochure to make an initial assessment about a certain type of holiday.

 ## Scan reading

Scan reading is similar to skimming in that you do not read the whole piece in depth. However, you do concentrate on certain parts of the document.

Scanning means you:

- read the title
- read the introduction or abstract
- look at pictures and charts
- look at references.

People might scan a bus timetable or a conference guide to find a particular section that they then read in more detail.

 ## Intensive reading

You use intensive reading if you need an in-depth knowledge of a subject, for example, John Bowlby's work on attachment.

This is the form of concentrated reading you should use to prepare for exams.

 ## Extensive reading

This means reading widely, often for pleasure. It could be the same as intensive reading if you are enjoying your research!

Benefits of reading for pleasure include:

- increased reading speed
- improved comprehension skills
- extended vocabulary
- better language skills (writing, speaking and listening skills).

Matching your technique to purpose

When completing your assessment tasks:

✓ you are likely to start by skimming or scanning literature, so you can find key information relating to your topic

✓ you would then adopt a more intensive reading style to identify key points within articles and understand the literature more deeply

✓ if there are concepts or ideas that interest or confuse, you might do some extensive reading to get a richer understanding of theories and previous research.

Highlighting and annotating

Some people find it helpful to use a highlighter pen to pick out important information when skimming, scanning or reading in more depth. An alternative is to underline important information. You might wish to jot brief notes in the margin. Obviously, you should only do this on your own copies of original documents!

Now try this

1 What is the difference between skimming and scanning?

2 When would you use these techniques?

 Skimming and scanning are skills that improve with practice.

Academic reading and analysis

When conducting and evaluating research, and in your assessment for this unit, you need to undertake academic reading and examine the content of secondary materials. The four key features below can be found in most pieces of current research. You can usually get a good idea of the key aspects of research from an initial skim read, especially of the opening and conclusion. You can then analyse each part in more detail.

 Introductions and abstracts

Where an abstract is included, this is an overall summary of the research piece. This is often followed by an introduction. Most openings of a piece of research introduce:

- **what** the study explored
- **how** it explored it
- the **participants**
- the **key findings**
- **recommendations** for future research
- its impact on **policy/practice/provision (the 3 Ps)**.

 Research methodology

Most pieces of research have a section on **methods**. This might also be called **research design** or **study design**. It tells you about:

- **design methods** used, e.g. qualitative, quantitative or mixed methods
- **definitions** of key terms
- **data collection** used, e.g. focus groups, questionnaires, interviews, observations
- **data analysis** used, e.g. analysis of previous findings and comparisons, explanatory model and categories.

 Results

Most pieces of research have a section on **results** that includes:

- **key research findings**, which are presented without being interpreted. Findings are based on methodologies used to gather information. Presentation may include use of tables and diagrams
- **discussion**, e.g. what the findings illustrate, relationship to other research, implications for practice, limitations and strengths.

 Conclusions

Most **conclusions** to a piece of research will give you:

- a **summary** of the study
- the **overall** and **key findings**
- **recommendations** for future research
- **strengths** and **limitations** of the research
- impact on **policy/practice/provision**.

 Reference list / bibliography

A reference list/bibliography is provided at the end of the article that includes sources referred to in the research, or sources read as part of the research.

Links See pages 119–120 for information on referencing conventions and techniques.

Now try this

Undertake a quick internet search for current research articles around a topic of your choice. Look at the structure of the articles. Choose one and find:

(a) the abstract/introduction
(b) the research methodologies
(c) the results
(d) the conclusions
(e) the references/bibliography.

Referencing conventions

You have to understand and be able to use referencing conventions and techniques. You will be expected to compile bibliographies and reference lists and present them correctly, using academically accepted conventions.

References and bibliographies

These list the **literature** that the writer has read and **cited** (mentioned) in their work.

- A **reference** section lists all the sources that have been cited in a text.
- A **bibliography** takes the same format as a reference list but lists everything you read about the topic, not only the sources you have mentioned in your written work.

Correct referencing is important.

- You should always acknowledge the source of any information (**plagiarism** is using information without correct attribution).
- Good referencing increases the validity of your work as it shows that other researchers have published supporting information.
- The reader should be able to access any source material that you used – good referencing will help them find your sources easily.
- If you know how to read reference lists, you will always be able to find more references around a topic of interest.

Following conventions

Be aware when reading texts that some authors may use the terms 'references' and 'bibliography' differently. The definitions in this book are conventionally accepted ways of using the two terms.

Referencing systems

There are a number of different referencing systems, the most widely used being the Harvard system, which is followed in this guide (see page 120). In your assessment you will need to list your references on the first page of your taskbook using an academic reference system. Whatever referencing system is used, it must be used consistently and correctly throughout.

Notation system – footnotes

When reading texts you need to understand the **notation system**, which is a small superscript number inserted next to the relevant text, like this[1].

1 Authors give the reference as a **footnote** at the bottom of the page, preceded by the matching number. Footnotes are often given in smaller text.

Notation system – endnotes

Endnotes[2] are referenced in a list at the end of the section of text.

2 An endnote looks very much like a footnote.

Whether footnotes or endnotes are used, there will also be a **full reference list** at the end of the work.

Plagiarism

Plagiarism is quoting other people's work without giving them credit. You can fail some courses for plagiarism. To avoid plagiarism, you must cite and reference correctly.

✓ You can use quote marks to show that you have used someone else's words, and you must include the reference, for example: *Galotti (2011, p. 400) states that the analytic system is 'more deliberate and explicit'*...

✓ You can paraphrase (use your own words) and provide a reference, for example: *Galotti compares the analytic and the experiential systems (2011, p.400).*

Now try this

1 Why is it important to cite references correctly, whether within the text or in reference lists?

2 What is the difference between a reference section and a bibliography?

Referencing techniques

You will need to understand and use a conventional referencing system for articles and books. A widely used referencing system is known as the Harvard system.

Referencing journal articles

Here is an example of a reference for a journal article.

> Hackett, A. (2014) 'Movement and emerging literacy', *Early Education Journal*, No 74, pp. 4–5.

The information appears in the following order.

- Author (last name first) and initial
- Date
- Title of article
- *Journal title*
- Volume (and issue number)
- Page numbers.

Note how the name of the journal appears in *italics*. In handwritten references using this style, you underline the title of the journal. The use of punctuation, such as full stops, commas and brackets is also important.

Referencing a book

Here is an example of a reference for a book.

> Sacks, O. (2011) *The Man Who Mistook His Wife for a Hat.* London: Picador.

The information appears in the following order.

- Author (last name first) and initial
- Date
- *Book title*
- Place of publication: publisher.

Note how the book name appears in *italics*. Always use a colon (:) between the place of publication and the publisher's name.

Citing references in text

This is how you would cite a reference in the body of your work:

Hackett (2014) argues that as literacy depends on place and context, children are likely to employ a range of different methods to communicate.

OR

Current research suggests that as literacy depends on place and context, children are likely to employ a range of different methods to communicate (Hackett, 2014).

Multiple authors

This is how you would cite a reference by more than one author.

Bryant and Bradley (1985:24) argue that the educationalists are not...

OR

Some research argues that educationalists need to do more (Bryant & Bradley, 1985, p.24).

> Note that an ampersand (&) is used in the brackets but 'and' is written out in full in the main text.

If there are three authors, give all names: Clark, Kemp and Howarth (2016, p.189) argue that... If there are four or more authors, give the name of the first author, followed by *et al* which means 'and others': Jones et al (2016, p.189) argue that...

Referencing online information

You need to reference electronic sources carefully because websites change and you may need to find the information elsewhere. If you are referring to a web document or journal, use the systems described above. After the publisher, or instead if there isn't a publisher, give the name of the website of the organisation responsible for providing/maintaining the information: http://internetaddress/remotepath, and the date it was accessed in square brackets, as in the following example.

Trodd, L. *Transitions in the Early Years.* [e-book] SAGE Publications. Available: http://www.ebooks.com/1110140/transitions-in-the-early-years/trodd-lyn/ [19 May 2016].

Now try this

Choose any book and reference it using a conventional system.

You could use the guide above. Make sure that you include the correct information, punctuation and italic (or underlined) text.

Selecting reliable research

When searching for sources of research into a contemporary early years issue, you need to select **reliable** sources.

Reliable publications

Sources of reliable secondary research include:

- professional journals, e.g. *The Early Education Journal*
- textbooks
- periodicals such as *Nursery World*.

Reputable journals and publishers of academic books often use peer review. This is where experts scrutinise and review articles prior to publication, so there is confidence in the reliability of the sources included.

Reliable organisations

Sources of reliable secondary research also include:

- professional bodies, e.g. the National Association for the Education of Young Children
- organisations involved in research, e.g. Department for Education, local authorities, social services departments, children's charities, e.g. NSPCC, the Office for National Statistics (ONS).

Reliable sources

When searching for reliable sources, consider these questions.

- Where does the information come from?
- Who provided the information – are they expert in their field?
- What was the motivation for the research? (E.g. is there any bias in the reporting?)
- Is the source reliable? (E.g. some institutions advise against using Wikipedia as it may not be considered a reliable source, as information can be given or edited by anyone at any time. Any errors may, or may not, be noticed.)
- Is the information consistent with other research? A single study is not enough to prove a point or make a case.

- Has the source of the funding for the research influenced the findings?
- Where was it published? In a reliable peer reviewed journal or in someone's blog, so based on opinion rather than fact?
- Is the internet site provided by an official body, organisation or authoritative source?

Contemporary sources

When selecting sources for this unit, they should be contemporary. This usually means that the research has taken place during the last 10 years.

Advantages and limitations of sources

When considering the findings of research from any source, carefully consider any wide **generalisations** made about children and their families. Huge and representative samples are needed for valid generalisations. Even then, findings might only apply to sections of the population, not to everyone. Research articles often state the limitations of the research, including the size of the sample.

👍 One advantage of research articles is that you can judge the reliability of generalisations based on the sample they use. The more representative of the population they are, the more valid and reliable they become.

👎 One limitation is that they often don't allow access to the actual data findings are based on, so you only have the generalisations, or conclusions, to work from.

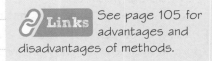 Links   See page 105 for advantages and disadvantages of methods.

See page 105 for advantages and disadvantages of methods.

Now try this

1. What is meant by 'peer review'?
2. How would you establish whether a piece of research is 'contemporary'?
3. What is one way of considering whether generalisations in a piece of research are reliable?

Electronic searches

When searching to select appropriate secondary sources, getting the literature search right can save you hours of time. Conducting **electronic searches effectively** by narrowing the range of information to a manageable size will help to produce a good-quality piece of work.

Refining electronic searches

When using a search engine you could use simple **internet keyword searches**, e.g.

Partnership   Working together   Early years collaboration

You can also **refine your search data**. Here are five ways, for example.

1 **Use quote marks** to search for an exact phrase to stop the search engine giving you every source that has the words in the phrase but not in the same order, for example:

'early childhood education'.

2 **Use a plus sign** or the word **AND** to narrow a search by combining terms. The following examples will find information about both literacy and key stage 1.

literacy + key stage 1   literacy AND key stage 1

> Be aware that different search engines and **library databases** use different protocols, such as the symbol + or the word AND, so use help screens to find out.

3 **Use a minus sign** or the word **NOT** to eliminate words from your search. The following example will give you facts about outdoor play without forest schools.

outdoor play – forest schools   outdoor play not forest schools

4 **Use the word OR** to broaden a search to include results that contain either of the words you type in, for example:

nursery or kindergarten

5 **If you use * after a word** it will bring up all possible extensions of the word. For example, if you enter partner*, the search engine will bring up partner, partnerships and partners.

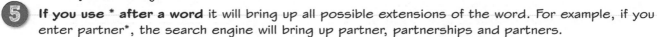

Targeting your search

You can **limit** and **refine** your searches by date, language, place of publication, author, publication or document type. A search engine such as Google has toolbars and menus for this purpose. For example:

- **Search tools** allow the user to restrict the search results to those published in a particular country or during a time span.
- **Books** restricts the search findings to publications.
- Options such as **Images** can be useful.

These might also be of use.

- **Google Scholar** refines searches to find journal articles.
- **Academic websites** – for example, some institutions have an **Athens** account, which provides access to all the sites that your institution has subscribed to, and allows access to e-resources.

Reading **abstracts** of articles can also be a quick and efficient method to help establish the reliability of sources and how far they are relevant to your research.

Now try this

Find out how to search your library database and whether you can access any online journals.

> The Association for Professional Development in Early Years (TACTYC) (www.tactyc.org.uk) would be one good online source for your work.

Connecting sources

As part of your research skills and assessment of this unit, you need to make connections and show the relationship between sources of information.

Making connections

You need to be able to connect your sources of information to each other and to your research project. When you conduct a search online, e.g. for data on children who have a child protection plan, this will generate numerous pieces of different information.

Think critically about each piece and consider the following.

* How exactly does this piece of information fit into my project?
* Does a source of information contribute a piece of the story to my project?
* How is it significant?
* How is it relevant to the big picture?
* What information is still missing?

Drawing conclusions

This means using simple coding and thematic analysis to find themes, patterns and relationships between sets of data.

Think critically about each piece. Do the data:

* show causation (that one thing is causing another)?
* show association (that one thing is related to another)?
* show differences (that one set of data is not related to another)?
* show what has been learned?
* support or disprove your hypothesis/idea/theory? If so, how? If not, why not?

Making connections and showing the relationship between your sources helps to result in a piece of research that is **reliable** and **valid**. It strengthens the argument, rationale and conclusions for your research.

Now try this

1 Name **two** things you need to think critically about when reviewing sources of information.
2 Why is it important to make connections between sources?

Suitability of sources

You need to assess the suitability of secondary sources for research, to establish their reliability and validity. One way is to evaluate the **S**ource, **A**ppearance, **M**ethods, **T**imeliness, **A**pplicability, **B**alance (SAMTAB) and also to consider the ethical principles applied to the research.

S – **Source:** Does it come from a reputable source/journal (usually noted on the web page)? Is author information included? Do you know the publisher? Note that Wikipedia may not always be a reliable source.

A – **Appearance:** Can you read and understand it? Is it professionally written (e.g. correct spelling and grammar)? Some sources may not be reliable as you may not know the author credentials.

M – **Methods:** Does it use appropriate and clear methods for the study? How big is the study? (E.g. a larger sample is more likely to be representative of the population; if it is smaller, it may be difficult to generalise more widely.) Do the research methods support reliability of results?

T – **Timeliness:** Is it up to date? It is best practice to find up-to-date material, e.g. from the past 10 years. Anything older may not be so reliable as society, thinking and research changes. Some old sources retain relevance, e.g. Piaget's cognitive theories of the 1960s.

A – **Applicability:** Does it focus on the issues/questions you are exploring? Research may be interesting but not necessarily relevant to the area being explored. If so, it will not add value.

B – **Balance:** Does it give an objective view or adopt a particular standpoint? If the opinions are not backed up by research, they may be biased, instead of substantiated fact.

Ethical principles checklist

Consider the suitability of sources in relationship to ethical considerations, where known.

☑ Have **ethical principles** been followed or referred to in the course of the research?

☑ Have parents and/or other participants given their **informed consent**?

☑ Has the author **fairly represented** the participants? If not, the author has behaved unethically.

☑ Has **confidentiality** of participants been respected and safeguarded?

☑ Has the author noted any potential **conflicts of interest** and how these were addressed, or suggested how these could affect the findings? If not, have you any concerns about conflicts of interest?

Selection for literature review

In your research and assessment when you evaluate sources, you should consider:

☑ sources of reliable research (page 121)

☑ how the sources relate to each other (page 123)

☑ the suitability of different methods used to research an issue e.g. qualitative (feelings), quantitative (numbers) or a mixture of both, and the reliability of results (page 123, pages 103–105)

☑ ethical principles (pages 108–113).

> **Links** Look at page 116 to revise keeping notes and records of sources, pages 119–120 to revise referencing techniques, and pages 135–137 for information on assessment and sources.

By answering questions such as those in the SAMTAB list, and using an ethical principles checklist, you can assess whether each article you find is worthy of being included in your literature review. When carrying out a literature review as part of your assessment of Unit 4, you need to match the criteria given for the research as noted in the task brief you will be given.

Now try this

Search for an article about an early years issue of your choice. Use the SAMTAB approach and ethical principles checklist to help assess its suitability.

Interpreting quantitative data

You need to understand how data have been treated in the research papers that you read, so that you can judge the significance of results for yourself. This is an important skill in research and in your assessment for this unit, where you need to analyse data provided, interpret the data and evaluate any quantitative conclusions drawn by the authors of the research.

Using quantitative analysis

The aim of quantitative analysis is to use numbers and **statistics** to describe a sample, in order to highlight any **significant differences** or **significant similarities** between two sample groups, or between the sample and the population.

Keywords

The following key words can be associated with quantitative analysis.

Correlation – a relationship or connection

Causation – when one thing brings about another

Dependent variable – a value that depends on another (usually the y-axis on a graph)

Independent variable – a value that doesn't depend on another (usually the x-axis on a graph)

Frequency – the number of times something occurs

Raw data – data gathered before analysis

Mean – average value obtained by adding the data set together and dividing by the number in the set

Median – the middle number in a set that is arranged in numerical order

Mode – the most common value in the set

Standard deviation – a test to discover how much a data set varies from the mean

Organising raw data

The first step in analysing quantitative data is organising the raw data to check completeness and accuracy. Notice if any data points are outside the expected range (**outliers**).

Tables could be used, or there are many **software packages** that can help organise and interpret data. **Spreadsheets** can be used to record and sort data, make calculations for data analysis and draw graphs in various formats.

Tables

Tables can be a useful way to organise data, for example:

Children with English as a second language			
Year	Rec	Year 1	Year 2
2014	4	2	2
2015	6	3	2
2016	7	5	4

Analysing data

Analysing data means interpreting the information and presenting it in a meaningful way.

Statistics are often used to investigate the significance of results, giving an indication of the likelihood that a difference in two data sets could be caused by chance alone.

Now try this

1   Organise the following data set.

2   Are there any outliers? If so, exclude them from your analysis.

3   Identify the mean, mode and median.

    4, 2, 9, 12, 6, 7, 11, 11, 2, 42, 5, 9, 6, 11, 14, 12

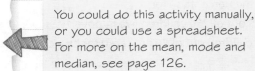

You could do this activity manually, or you could use a spreadsheet. For more on the mean, mode and median, see page 126.

125

Interpreting graphs and tables

You will need to understand how to interpret data from graphs and tables shown in research you have sourced. Here are some examples of the more common ones you may come across.

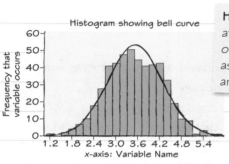

Histograms are useful at giving a good idea of the overall results as well as the mean and range.

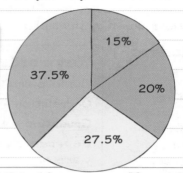

aged birth to 12 months ☐ aged 2 to 3 years
aged 12 months to 2 years ☐ aged 3 to 4 years

Pie charts are a goo graphical form to display data and give you an overall pictur of findings. They are often used to show data sets that are parts of a whole, such as percentages.

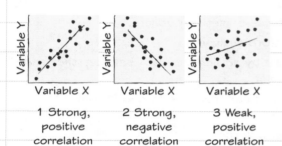

1 Strong, positive correlation

2 Strong, negative correlation

3 Weak, positive correlation

Scatter plots can be used to show the relationship or **correlation** between two variables.

Comparing outdoor play choices in a nursery setting

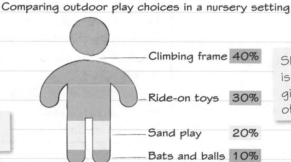

Climbing frame 40%

Ride-on toys 30%

Sand play 20%

Bats and balls 10%

Showing **percenta** is another way of giving a good pict of overall results.

Mean, mode, median, range

These are four terms often found together in statistics, giving you a good range of information.

1 **Mean:** add all the numbers together and divide by the number of numbers.

13 + 18 + 12 + 10 + 12 + 10 + 17 + 10 + 16 ÷ 9 = 13 (rounded)

2 **Median:** the middle value in the set when it is rearranged in numerical order.

10 10 10 12 12 13 16 17 18

Note that for equal numbers in a row (e.g. 10) you would take the middle two numbers.

3 **Mode:** the number that appears most often.

10 10 10 12 12 13 16 17 18

In this list, the mode is 10.

4 **Range:** the difference between the lowest and highest number.

The difference between 10 and 18 = 8.

Now try this

Find the percentage for:

(a) 45 out of 250 children live in poverty

(b) 7 children out of 70 are cared for by a childminder.

To work out a percentage, you divide the number by the total number and then multiply by 100, e.g. 35 balls bounced out of 200: 35 ÷ 200 x 100 = 17.5%

Bias in quantitative data

Bias can result from poorly planned research, and misuse of statistics can misrepresent results. You need to know about sources of bias and be aware of how statistics can be misused.

Sources of bias

 Leading questions

A leading or **loaded** question makes it more likely that a respondent will answer in a certain way, leading to bias in the results.

The proper way to conduct research is to ask **non-leading** questions. Here are examples of leading and non-leading questions.

- **Leading question**: Was your experience of treatment good?
- **Non-leading question**: How was your experience of treatment?

 Sample bias

Researchers may find they are not able to collect data equally from each sample, leading to some samples being under-represented and some samples being over-represented. For example, it may be very difficult to access samples of some sections of the population, such as families in poverty or children with a protection plan.

Misuse of data

 Sample size and generalisations

Small samples may be **non-representative** and could give **unreliable** data. For example, consider the statement: *98% of parents believe educational standards have dropped in the last 10 years.* 98% of what? You could generalise from 98% of 10 000 people but not from 98% of 10 people.

2 Validity

It may be true to say that 80% of dentists recommend FreshBrite toothpaste. But is the statement actually **valid** if dentists were asked to recommend three brands of toothpaste?

3 Selective use of data

A researcher may be selective in their use of data, picking out information that supports their argument and making vague or dismissive statements about data that do not.

> 🔗 **Links** Look at page 106 to revise open and closed questions, page 107 for sampling, page 113 for bias and page 121 for generalisations.

Recognising bias in graphs, tables and statistics

To recognise bias, be aware that:
- the scale on the axes of graphs can be manipulated to make data look more or less significant
- a table of selected data might give a false impression
- bias in statistics can occur through poor questioning, or use of an inappropriate sampling method or research method.

Risk of bias and misuse of data

Evidence-based policymaking uses research results to guide a government's policies. When research is carried out correctly, evidence-based policymaking has advantages. However, the implications of changing policy and practice based on biased, incorrect or untruthful research results are huge.

The Wakefield–MMR case (page 109) shows how incorrect research results can influence the public, causing changes to behaviour.

Now try this

Devise a leading question and non-leading question on the same early years topic. Predict how the leading question could influence the answers you would receive. If your question was part of a wider study, how could your biased findings influence policy or practice?

Interpreting qualitative data

You need to understand how to interpret qualitative data in research and also in source material that you read, so that you can judge the significance of results for yourself.

Qualitative versus quantitative

Interpreting qualitative data is very different from interpreting quantitative data. It involves making sense of what people **say and do**, rather than finding meaning in numbers.

Making sense of qualitative data is sometimes called **interpretive** research (as the researcher has to deduce the meaning in the participants' responses), whereas using numbers and statistics can give **definitive** results.

Qualitative data

The researcher makes transcripts of interviews and recordings, uses responses from open-ended surveys and questionnaires, analyses case studies and makes observations of behaviour. This produces largely unstructured data that have to be analysed.

One person's observation may be very different from another's. To analyse the observations, the researcher has to identify **common themes**.

Approaches to analysis

Different research skills are used when interpreting qualitative data. Here are some examples.

1   **Analysing transcripts**

Researchers analyse data from transcripts and make notes using:

 skim and scan reading skills to identify patterns and trends in people's words – highlighter pens are useful for **coding** different **themes**

 software such as NVivo supports analysis of unstructured data.

Be aware that interpretation of data may depend on a researcher's perspective and, as such, may be open to bias.

🔗 **Links**   See page 129 to revise more on coding and page 130 for more on bias.

2   **Identifying themes**

Analysis of transcripts involves looking for repeating themes in data. This might be carried out manually or using technology. These themes may emerge from the data (**inductive**) or start with an idea or theory (**deductive**).

3   **Inductive approach**

 'Bottom up' approach

 Theory emerges from the research

Research → Patterns → Tentative conclusions → Theory

4   **Deductive approach**

 'Top down' approach

 Starts with an idea or theory

 Results confirm or challenge original theory

Theory → Hypothesis → Research → Confirmation of hypothesis

Now try this

1   Why is interpreting qualitative data different from interpreting quantitative data?

2   What research skills do you need to analyse qualitative data?

Interpreting words

Interpreting qualitative data involves using research skills to interpret language data, distinguish between fact and opinion, and identify bias.

Distinguishing between fact and opinion

Researchers need to distinguish between fact and opinion.

- A **fact** is something that has actually happened or that is true and can be supported by evidence.
- An **opinion** is a belief, so can vary based on a person's perspective, emotions or individual understanding of something.

When you interpret language data you need to take an objective and non-judgemental approach, and identify bias. A professional journal is likely to contain mainly facts. A blog or Twitter may contain mainly opinion.

Analysing data

Transcribing, coding and interpreting qualitative data is a time-consuming process, which requires patience and organisation. Here are some approaches.

1 **Interpreting information**

Qualitative data include information about people's feelings and experiences, opinions and knowledge, expressed in their own words.

The researcher needs to:

☑ transcribe data word by word (**verbatim**)

☑ interpret **non-verbal** communication

☑ **code and categorise** sections of text

☑ understand what was said and deduce what was meant.

2 **Coding and categorising**

Coding or categorising data is an important aspect of analysing qualitative data. It involves subdividing large amounts of raw data and assigning these portions to **categories**.

☑ **Codes** are tags or labels for allocating portions of text to different themes, trends or patterns. Numbers and colours make useful coding systems.

☑ **Coded sections** are reorganised to bring text with similar themes together.

The researcher is looking for repeated patterns that will show connections between the sources of information in the data.

3 **Using different types of analysis**

Content	Used with verbal or behaviour data, to classify or summarise
Narrative	Used to transcribe experiences
Discourse	Used to understand everyday usage of language (spoken and written text)
Framework	Includes transcribing, reading, identifying themes, coding by theme, interpreting
Grounded theory	Inductive method for examining a single case, generating a theory, examining the next case and revising theory

Now try this

1. Ask three friends about their experiences of their early education. Have these been positive or negative experiences? As a result, how do they feel regarding their work in an early years setting?

2. Are there common themes and connections that you can identify in the three interviews? Be aware of what is fact, what is opinion, and take an objective standpoint.

Bias in qualitative data

Sources of bias, error and misuse

Sources of bias that are common to qualitative and quantitative data collections include:

- leading questions
- sample bias.

There are some additional sources of bias in relation to qualitative data which are due to:

- the interpersonal nature of the data-collection process
- distinguishing between fact and opinion.

Links See page 127 to revise bias in quantitative data and page 129 to revise fact and opinion and bias.

Recognising bias, error and misuse

A key research skill is the ability to identify potential sources of bias, error or misuse of data in literature, methods, analysis and conclusions of research. Here are some examples.

 Researcher bias

The researcher personally impacts on the quality of data. Body language, facial expression, tone of voice and style of language, dress, social status, race and gender can all influence the responses that participants may give.

Researcher body language can influence responses. An open and relaxed questioner will receive different responses from someone who is tense and hurried, or aggressive in their questioning.

 Respondent bias

Here are some examples of respondent bias.

✓ **Acquiescence bias** – when respondents tend to agree with the researcher or change their responses on the basis of what they think the researcher expects.

✓ **Dominant participant bias** – this may occur in a focus group situation, when a dominant personality influences the responses from the other group members.

✓ **Social desirability bias** – when respondents give a response that is socially acceptable to make them look good, rather than being truthful.

✓ **Mood bias** – The participant's own mood at the time of questioning can influence results.

Changing the way data is gathered can reduce respondent bias. For example, social bias can be reduced by allowing respondents to complete the survey anonymously or by guaranteeing confidentiality.

3 **Conformity error**

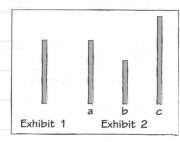

Exhibit 1   Exhibit 2

The Asch line judgement conformity study is a good example. In a group situation, the experimental subject was asked to match the line in Exhibit 1 to one of the lines in Exhibit 2. The aim of the study was to see which line the subject would choose if all members of the group had already given the same, obviously wrong answer. The tendency is to conform!

Misuse of qualitative data

Owing to the more subjective nature of qualitative data, it can be easy to misinterpret research findings. Findings may also be misrepresented, just as results from quantitative data can, and the risks of doing so are the same.

Now try this

1. How can researcher bias affect data collection?
2. Give an example of respondent bias.

 Links To revise non-judgemental practice, see page 113.

Recommendations for practice

Findings from research lead to recommendations for changes to working practice. Improving practice in early years settings helps to provide the best possible education and care for children and their families.

Research aims

Research in the early years sector aims to:

- improve outcomes for children and their families
- improve working practice by informing policy and procedures
- extend knowledge and understanding.

Research into working practice

Research into early years practice can provide positive improvements in working practices. From time to time, your professional body may change its code of practice or advice to professionals based on the findings of research. You should be aware of any developments in your field.

 Links See pages 98–100 to revise the purposes of research and issues in the early years sector.

The research cycle

This is how the research cycle can be applied to research into early years practice.

1 Research question

2 Research and findings

3 Learning

4 Implementation in practice

5 Reflection on skills and development for practice

Research log

Developments in research will guide parts of your professional development during your working life. It will be good practice to keep a log where you can record learning and its impact on your professional practice. You can also record any research that has an impact on your practice.

Now try this

1 How can current research support your continuing professional development to improve practice?

2 How do you intend to keep up to date with developments in your field?

Many workplaces have a subscription to a professional journal to enable practitioners to keep up to date. Your professional body will also publish relevant articles on research findings in their magazine or on their website.

Recommendations for provision

Findings from research lead to recommendations and potential for changes to the provision of early years care and educational services, improving outcomes for children and their families.

Implications for provision

Research leads to an understanding of:

- gaps in provision
- ways to improve provision
- access to provision.

This is carried out by:

- the Department for Education (DfE)
- National Foundation for Educational Research (NFER)
- universities
- charities.

Improving outcomes for children

An example of research leading to change in provision and improving outcomes for children was carried out by Professor Cathy Nutbrown for the Department for Children, Schools and Families (now the Department for Education) in 2011.

- The research showed that the present qualifications for the early years workforce were not equipping practitioners with the knowledge and skills they needed to provide high-quality care and education (Nutbrown, 2011).
- This led to the introduction of quality qualifications at level 3 that meet 'full and relevant' early years educator criteria.
- As the workforce becomes more skilled it will lead to best practice and provision that leads to improved experiences and outcomes for children.

Benefits to provision

Some research findings show the benefits of early years provision for the whole family.

For example, Oxford University published the report 'The impact of children's centres: studying the effects of children's centres in promoting better outcomes for young children and their families' (Sammons et al, 2015). The report concludes that children's centres can have an impact on family functioning and parenting, and that services are highly valued by parents. It was also found that children's centres provide for families with greater need but may not always be able to provide for their complex needs. This has implications for how the needs of families are identified and for wider provision of children's services.

Research findings can inform practice and provision in early years services. This supports practitioners in the early years sector who can then target specific resources to benefit children and their families.

Now try this

Look at a few pieces of research you have identified that consider provision. Taking an objective standpoint, assess the possible effects on outcomes of children and their families.

Links See pages 98–100 to revise the purposes of research and issues in early years.

Identifying future research

Evaluation of research findings often identifies potential areas for development of the research. It can also lead to further potential areas for research by posing further questions.

Potential for further research

An example of research that made recommendations for changes in practice and suggested further research is: 'Positive beginnings? The role of the Key Person in Early Years adult-child relationships', submitted to the University of Exeter by Lemos, M. in 2012. The research drew on other research on the role of the key person, which is a statutory requirement of the EYFS. The researcher identified implications for early years settings that could lead to further study around the role of the key person.

Findings and recommendations

Key findings and recommendations from the research were as follows.

- Key persons used experience in carrying out their role rather than basing practice on theoretical understanding.
- Understanding of the key person role varied across settings.
- Key person allocations were often made on the basis of staff rotas so became an 'administrative' role.
- Children interact more frequently with their key person than other adults, particularly those children with social or emotional needs.

Potential areas for further research

The research could be developed in areas such as:

- the effectiveness of early years qualifications to prepare practitioners for the role of the key person
- how early years settings collaborate to share experiences and organisation of the role of key persons
- the key person role from the perspective of children and their families
- the effectiveness of the key person role in the early identification of additional needs.

Potential for development of practice and provision

The research into the key person role could potentially lead to:

- changes in policy and procedures in the setting around the allocation (or reallocation) of children to key persons
- a better understanding of how relationships are formed between practitioners and children
- development of a more effective key person role
- consistency in practice within and across different types of setting
- earlier recognition and intervention for children with additional needs.

Benefits of research

In relation to the above study, it is possible to generalise about the benefits of doing such research.

- Staff are better prepared to take on the role.
- It encourages reflective practice.
- Strategies for building effective relationships are developed.
- It leads to greater collaboration between colleagues and settings.
- Professionalism within the workforce increases.
- It leads to better training and career progression.
- Outcomes for children are improved.

Now try this

Look at the main findings from this research. What areas for further research would you recommend?

You can see clearly how the findings from this study can:
- lead to recommendations
- pose further questions for research
- suggest changes in provision
- influence policy.

Reflecting on research

Before moving on to look at the skills you will need in your assessment of this unit, it is useful to reflect on both the importance of doing research and your role in the research process.

Your role

Your role is important in the research process.

- As a **practitioner**, you know how research can make a difference to practice, provision and children's development and well-being. You can use research findings to improve your own personal practice and encourage others to do the same.

- As a **researcher**, you can formulate your research questions to have positive impacts in your own setting.

Your aims

You might undertake research to:

1. find out new knowledge

2. discover new ways of doing things

3. understand things – cognitive development, health conditions, children's behaviours, why rewards work and don't work

4. make a positive impact on policy, practice and/or children's outcomes.

Now try this

What are you good at? What do you need to work at? Rate your abilities with each of the skills below. Use any system you like – a number score, traffic light system, or just make notes about what you need to do to improve and revise with the pages shown.

To be an effective researcher, you should have the skills to:

(a) understand the purpose, issues and rationale for research (revise pages 98–102)

(b) use time management techniques, organisational skills and understand triangulation (revise page 101)

(c) identify and use research methods, questions and target groups (revise pages 103–107)

(d) identify and carry out ethical practice (revise pages 108–112)

(e) identify and implement an objective standpoint (revise page 113)

(f) be able to make notes and keep records from source material (revise pages 114–116)

(g) use a variety of reading techniques, such as skimming and scanning (revise page 117)

(h) understand the conventions of academic writing, including introduction, methodology, results and conclusion, and presenting bibliography and reference lists (revise pages 118–120)

(i) select key sources and identify features of this literature (revise pages 121–122, page 124)

(j) show connections between reliable sources of information (revise page 123)

(k) analyse data using valid methods, including compilation of data, results and findings, interpret graphs and tables, use percentages and statistical averages, select relevant numerical data and draw conclusions (revise pages 125–126)

(l) be critical, picking up on bias or misuse of data, assessing the validity of generalisations and distinguishing between fact and opinion (revise pages 127–129).

Notice that these are also the skills you need to possess in order to use research to become an effective practitioner!

Your Unit 4 set task

Unit 4 will be assessed through a task, which will be set by Pearson. You will be given a current piece of research into early years and asked to carry out your own secondary research related to the issue. You will use your understanding of the methodologies of contemporary research, apply your knowledge of early years educational issues, and investigate the implications for early years practice.

Revising your skills

Your assessed task could cover any of the essential content in the unit. You can revise the unit content in this Revision Guide. This skills section is designed to **revise skills** that might be needed in your assessed task. The section uses selected content and outcomes to provide an example of ways of applying your skills.

Research implications for future provision and practice (see pages 148-149)

Planning research (see an example on page 136)

Finding current research sources (see an example on page 137)

Making notes (see an example on page 138)

Planning and ethical considerations for further research (see pages 145-147)

Set task skills

Listing sources (see an example on page 139)

Understanding the relationship between your own secondary research and the provided piece of research, and how this relationship reinforces the importance of the issue (see pages 143-144)

Understanding research methods and the validity and reliability of results in research (see pages 140-142)

Workflow

The process of undertaking and responding to current research might follow these steps:

- ✓ Read and analyse the provided current research piece
- ✓ Plan and carry out your own related independent secondary research, using current secondary sources
- ✓ Make notes and links on key areas of focus
- ✓ List sources
- ✓ Respond to activities in relation to the provided research and your own related secondary research

Check the Pearson website

The activities and sample response extracts in this section are provided to help you to revise content and skills. Ask your tutor or check the Pearson website for the most up-to-date **Sample Assessment Material** and **Mark Scheme** to get an indication of the structure of your actual assessed task and what this requires of you. The details of the actual assessed task may change so always make sure you are up to date.

Now try this

Visit the Pearson website and find the page containing the course materials for BTEC National Children's Play, Learning and Development. Look at the latest Unit 4 Sample Assessment Material for an indication of:

- The structure of your set task, and whether it is divided into parts
- How much time you are allowed for the task, or different parts of the task
- What briefing or stimulus material might be provided to you
- Any notes you might have to make and whether you are allowed to take selected notes into your supervised assessment
- The activities you are required to complete and how to format your responses.

Planning research

Here are some examples of skills involved in planning research. The plan shows one way of breaking the research into stages.

Sample notes extract

Read and annotate a piece of current research into early years.
Familiarise myself with the research piece, making notes and identifying issues.
Note key words for secondary research sources, to search on identified issues.
Search and create records of possible sources for secondary research best related to the issue in the provided research piece.
Assess reliability of secondary research sources, chosen with reference to **S**ource, **A**ppearance, **M**ethods, **T**imeliness, **A**pplicability and **B**alance (SAMTAB), ethical considerations and links in relationship to the issues in the provided research piece.

Make short bullet notes on secondary research sources under six headings, also noting the relationship to the provided article.

1 What was the research piece about? (E.g. what it explored, why important, what the study looked at to find out.)

2 What were the key methods used in the research and were they reliable? (E.g. qualitative, quantitative, mix of both; how they supported reliability of research.)

3 What were the key findings in the research? (E.g. What were the results of the study? Did they answer the research questions? conclusions of the research?)

4 Were any recommendations/future research plans discussed? (E.g. Do they recommend further research? Did any aspects of the research not go well? Consider proposal, methods, reliability, research skills required, ethical considerations, timescales.)

5 What could be the implications/impact on individual practice? (E.g. How can this type of research affect individuals in the workplace? How will it affect individual practice?)

6 What could the implications/impact be on service provision? (E.g. What is the impact on society? What are the implications for the cost and effectiveness of early years providers?)

- This plan breaks down the key stages of planning research in a detailed, clear and logical way. You need a plan that you can check progress against.
- This plan uses a method for searching, assessing and making notes in a structured way that brings together key information.

Now try this

Look at the Sample Assessment Material on the Pearson website and find out how much time is allowed for your research. Think about what is involved in the stages of research and make a note of estimated timings for each of the stages.

Finding sources

Here are some examples of skills involved in finding and assessing the relevance and validity of pieces of current secondary research. One way of doing this is to consider the **S**ource, **A**ppearance, **M**ethods, **T**imeliness, **A**pplicability, **B**alance (SAMTAB) and ethical principles of any piece of research.

Sample notes extract

Assessing reliability and validity of a source –
Source, **A**ppearance, **M**ethods, **T**imeliness, **A**pplicability, **B**alance (SAMTAB)

TITLE, AUTHOR, SOURCE

Use a referencing format (e.g. Harvard).

- Davy, A. (2016) 'Provision for Learning Outdoors for Under 5s: State of the Nation Survey', *Learning Through Landscapes and Early Childhood Forum* [Online] Available: www.earlychildhoodforum.org/uploads/EYFS_Outdoors_Final_Report.pdf [18 January 2016].

SOURCE

Does it come from a reputable source/journal (usually noted on the web page)? Is author information included? Do you know the publisher? Note that Wikipedia may not always be a reliable source.

- The sources, Learning Through Landscapes and Early Childhood Forum, are reputable.

APPEARANCE

Can you read and understand it? Does it look professionally written (e.g. correct spelling and grammar)? Some sources may not necessarily be reliable as you may not know the credentials of the author.

- Author is cited. The appearance of the website link, plus the article itself, looks authentic; information is contemporary and relevant.

METHODS

Does it use appropriate methods for the study? Are the methods clear? How big is the study? Do the research methods support reliability of results? Is the method similar to the provided article, or different?

- This article reports that a survey was adopted involving almost 400 respondents from across the UK.

- Of these, 83% were early years practitioners, while others had a close interest in childcare, including owners of childcare businesses, governors, childcare lecturers and parents.

- When assessing reliability, the method and sample size will need to be considered.

- In relationship to the provided article...

In this extract of notes assessing secondary sources, an appropriate source has been identified. You need to make brief notes as you assess sources, then expand notes on your chosen secondary sources. Your notes should make the relationship to the provided article clear.

Now try this

Search for a secondary research source related to provision for children under 5 years. Complete a SAMTAB and brief notes using the six headings: Source, Appearance, Methods, Timeliness, Applicability, Balance. Evaluate the source for ethical principles also.

Links Look at page 124 for a complete SAMTAB and an ethical principles checklist you can use when assessing suitability of sources.

Making notes

Here are some examples of skills involved when making notes. They relate to Garrick, R. et al (2010) *Children's experiences of the Early Years Foundation Stage*, Sheffield Hallam University (DFE-RB 071).

Sample notes extract

This extract from notes on methods includes detail you need to be clear about:
- method used
- how it was used
- participants (number and who)
- method purpose.
- make clear and focused notes.

What were the key methods used in the research and were they reliable?
- Research by Garrick et al (2010) used qualitative methods.
- Use of records of children's learning and development.
- Mosaic approach (combining traditional approaches of observation and interviews with activities such as 'My best day' to find out about play experiences and a floor mapping activity to understand relationships).
- Participatory rural appraisal techniques (bottom up approach that involves children to find their needs and their views of provision).
- Participant observations (a method involving getting close to the children as they experience their environment).
- 15 case studies (to look at children's experiences in different types of early years settings across two regions of England).
- Children and groups.

Sample notes extract

What were the key findings in the research
- <u>Children's experiences</u> varied in different types of setting.
- <u>The settings</u> generally met the needs of children in relation to the requirements of the EYFS but, by looking at provision from a child's point of view, omissions could be identified.
- <u>The play children most enjoyed</u> was usually linked to the area of learning Knowledge and Understanding of the World, with some children viewing play activities linked to numeracy as 'work'.

Planning:
- children were not always aware that their own interests were being taken into account in planning
- there was evidence that when practitioners engaged with children in their self-directed play, children's ideas were more likely to be involved in planning.

Physical activity:
- opportunities for physical activity is another area where there were differences between settings
- the type of play on offer outdoors was often restricted
- physically active play indoors was rarely mentioned except in a Steiner kindergarden
- although children showed that they enjoyed adult involvement in their play there were few references to their involvement in physical play.

In this extract from notes on key findings, the main results are clearly summarised.

You could use the article used in the SAMTAB on page 137 and the six headings in the plan on page 136.

Preparatory notes
You may be allowed to take some of your preparatory notes into your supervised assessment time. If so, there may be restrictions on the length and type of notes that are allowed. Check with your tutor or look at the most up-to-date Sample Assessment Material on the Pearson website for details.

Now try this

1 Examine the notes on this page. Explain why the quality of early years provision might be an important research issue.

2 Search for an appropriate secondary research source related to the quality of early years provision and make focused bullet notes.

Listing sources

Here are some examples of skills involved if you are asked to list research sources using a conventional referencing system (e.g. Harvard). In the skills pages that follow, the reference for the main article is Garrick, R. et al (2010) *Children's experiences of the Early Years Foundation Stage.* Sheffield Hallam University (DFE-RB 071).

Sample notes extract

Ayaga, G., Odongo, C., Ajowi, J. (2016) Implication of Preschool Outdoor Environment on Pupils' Learning: Facts on the importance of outdoor based curriculum in preschool pedagogy. Lambert: Academic Publishing.

 It is conventional to list your sources in alphabetical order.

 You need to use a conventional style to reference a book source, with the book title in italic or underlined.

Davy, A. (2016) 'Provision for Learning Outdoors for Under 5s: State of the Nation Survey', *Learning Through Landscapes and Early Childhood Forum.* [Online] Available: www.earlychildhoodforum.org/uploads/EYFS_Outdoors_Final_Report.pdf [18 April 2016].

 You need to use a conventional style to reference a source from the internet.

Grenier, J. (2015) 'First of All', <u>Nursery World</u>, June–July, pp. 40–41.

Sylva, K. et al (2004) 'The Effective Provision of Pre-school Education [EPPE] Project', The Institute of Education [Online] Available: http://eppe.ioe.ac.uk/eppe/eppepdfs/RBTec1223sept0412.pdf [21 April 2016].

 You need to use a conventional style to reference a journal article, with the journal title in italic or underlined, and the title of the article not in italic.

Wanderfelt R. and Blink, B. (2012) 'The Importance of Early Years Provision: Play and the Early Years Curriculum', *The Journal on Early Years Play*, 12 (2), pp. 24–29.

 NB: this last journal article reference is fictitious and has been used only to provide an example for the example responses.

Now try this

Carry out an internet search for one journal article, one book and one web page around the issue of the effectiveness of settings to support children's learning and well-being, and cite each one using a conventional style of reference.

 See pages 119–120 for more information on referencing. You can find guides on the internet for conventional ways of presenting references.

Research methods

Here are some examples of the skills involved when focusing on research methods.

For example, if focusing on what type of research methods have been used to extract data in a provided research piece and chosen secondary research sources about the issue, consider:

- other methods used to explore the issue
- how reliable the results of the research methods used are.

Methods used

Consideration of methods might include:

- ✓ qualitative, quantitative, mixed methods
- ✓ use of data to explore the issue
- ✓ the suitability of the research methods and how they support the reliability of the findings
- ✓ comment on any issues that may have affected the results.

Sample response extract

In the study conducted by Garrick, qualitative methods were used which included a mosaic approach, participatory rural appraisal techniques, observations and case studies.

 In this extract, referring to the provided article, you need to give a **full reference**. Only a brief reference is made here.

Improved response extract

Research conducted by Garrick et al (2010) is a study of children's experiences of the EYFS in different types of setting. The report drew on 15 case studies involving 146 advantaged and disadvantaged children across different types of setting.

Qualitative methods were used as the study focused on evidence from the children's own viewpoint. This meant the researchers used a 'bottom up' approach using participatory rural appraisal techniques, which involved close involvement of the researchers with the participants in their setting.

A mosaic approach, which involved the production of a picture book showing a child's ideal day in the setting and a mapping activity showing relationships, allowed researchers to analyse children's experiences from different perspectives.

 You need to go beyond stating methods. You should **explain** the methods used in the research (e.g. mosaic approach and participatory rural appraisal approach). You should include the number of **participants** and **explain** what they did.

 In this extract, referring to a provided article, a **full reference** is given.

 The number of **participants** are **identified**.

 More information is provided to help **understand** the methods.

 The response **explains** the mosaic approach and participatory rural appraisal techniques using improved **terminology**, outlining the **scope of research**.

Now try this

Choose a piece of research. Identify what methods were used for what purpose, the participants, and the sample type and size (for example, if a questionnaire was sent to a specified number of early years settings).

🔗 **Links** See pages 102–107 to revise research methods and target groups and samples.

Suitability of methods

Here are some examples of ways of explaining the suitability of research methods clearly, using the correct terminology.

Sample response extract

In another study conducted by Wanderfelt & Blithe, they used quantitative and qualitative methods. They used surveys on practitioners asking them to rate play opportunities for children in their early years setting. They also used interviews on parents to see how they perceived the importance of play for their children.

 In this extract the learner is referring to their own secondary research. You need to give a **correct and full** reference, but this reference is brief and incorrect (using the wrong name for one of the researchers).

 You need to **make clear** which are the qualitative and quantitative elements of the study, and why they are suitable. Here it is not clear.

Improved response extract

The study conducted by Wanderfelt and Blink (2012) used quantitative and qualitative methods (being a mixed methods design). For the quantitative element the survey asked participants to rate how play provision in their setting supports each of the areas of learning in the Early Years Foundation Stage using a Likert scale. This is a common method used, for example, using a scale of between 1 and 10. The qualitative aspect of the study comprised interviewing 10 parents of children attending the settings to find their views on how play can support their child's learning and development. The use of a Likert scale is good as it is often used so is recognisable and easily understood, easily quantifiable for analysis and does not require the participant to take a definite yes or no stand on the issue, although there might be a tendency for people not to pick the extremes of the scale, even if it is their most accurate answer.

 In this extract, referring to the learner's own secondary research, the learner **cites the source correctly**.

 It is clear that **quantitative** research was used. The response **explains** the methodology and its **suitability**, using **correct terminology**.

 The **qualitative** elements of the study are clear.

The response shows the learner knows the **advantages** and **disadvantages** of methods, such as a Likert scale.

Now try this

Using a source that you have identified, select a method of research and explain it in detail. Make sure you include **how** the method was used to explore the issue, and its suitability and reliability.

 Use the correct terminology for your methods and detailed explanations.

🔗 **Links** See pages 103–107 to revise research methods, advantages and disadvantages, and reliability.

Methods and reliability

Here are some examples of skills involved if assessing the reliability of research methods in a provided article and chosen related secondary sources.

Sample response extract

Because there were so many methods used in the study, it might be that the study is considered reliable. The authors used data from a large number of children across different types of setting.

In this extract on the **Garrick** research, the learner does not provide a reference for the research, which the reader needs. The learner gives a **basic** answer to the question of how **reliable the results** of the research methods used are, with limited information.

Improved response extract

The Garrick et al (2010) study included 146 children and 15 different settings. This helped the researcher to gather data to reach reliable conclusions about the experiences of pre-school. The range of data gathered included children from different family backgrounds (advantaged and disadvantaged) and sixteen settings. Using a triangulation of methods, as in this study, does help to make it more reliable. For example, researchers observed children closely in their play, listened to their comments and also used evidence from their picture book that illustrated what they enjoyed. Researchers considered evidence from different perspectives linked to the principles of the EYFS, which gave a rounded picture of children's experience in each setting, looking at the following.

The unique child – how well the setting met the needs of individual children.
Positive relationships – children's views on the importance of relationships.
Positive environment – how well the environment led to positive experiences.
The research does not include the views of disabled children so it is difficult to make a judgement on the overall inclusivity of setting for all children.

This extract provides a clear reference to the research study along with **detail** on how **reliable the learner feels the results** of the **research methods** to be. Answering in this way shows how well they understand the research aims of the study, its methods and results.

Sample response extract

This study only had a small sample so the results cannot be used to say with certainty that it would apply to all children.

In this extract on the **Wanderfelt and Blink** research, the learner has provided **basic information** about the **reliability of methods** that may suggest the results cannot be relied upon. The learner needs to clearly show how the methods used might be unreliable.

Improved response extract

Using a mix of qualitative and quantitative methods (mixed methods) is a good way to increase reliability of any research. However, the Wanderfelt and Blink (2012) research was based only on a small sample of 12 children and two types of setting so although the results can be useful in informing future research, they may not be reliable for making generalisations about outcomes for children from different family backgrounds and different types of setting as there was a limited range of responses.

This extract provides **detail** about the **reliability of methods** and **explains** what that might mean in terms of **usage and results**. Providing more detailed information shows how you understand the research aims of the study, its methods and results.

Now try this

Explain why using a triangulation of methods may help research results to be more reliable.

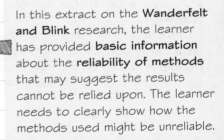

Links See pages 101, 103, 104, 105, 107 and 121 to revise triangulation, methods, reliability of results, samples and generalisations.

Research issues and significance

Here are some examples of skills involved if asked about the relationship between a provided research piece and chosen secondary research sources, and how the relationship reinforces the importance of the issue.

For example, if the provided research piece focuses on research that leads to a better understanding of the effectiveness of pre-school provision and why this is important to children's outcomes, you would include how far your secondary research supports the conclusions drawn in the provided research piece.

Importance of issues in research

When analysing research issues, leading to conclusions about an issue's **importance**:

- ✓ provide relevant **examples** of the effects on children's outcomes and **support** these from the research findings
- ✓ assess **how far** secondary research supports the conclusions of the provided research piece
- ✓ make an **objective** response, based on facts and examples from the research.

Sample response extract

This article was about how pre-school provision can meet the needs of children. Settings generally met the needs of children but there are variations.

In this extract, referring to the provided article, although the learner's outline and conclusions are correct, they do not provide much detail of the influences on children's outcomes.

Improved response extract

This article was aimed at gaining a better understanding of children's experiences in pre-school settings. Conclusions from Garrick et al (2010) have shown that children do have positive experiences in early years settings but there may be weaknesses in some settings. For example, children's views are not always taken into account when planning. Although children enjoyed learning through play they had less enjoyment in developing mathematical concepts through play. In some settings opportunities for active physical play were limited.

In this extract, referring to the provided article, the learner starts by providing an outline and conclusions of the article, making clear the intention of the study.

The extract provides an objective judgement that summarises the article's position.

Sample response extract

The Garrick et al study (2010) showed the importance of viewing the curriculum from the perspective of children. If practitioners engaged with children more in child-initiated play activities they would be more likely to understand their individual needs and interests. This could have implications for the way practitioners plan and assess children's learning.

The response goes on to say why the research in the provided article is important for improving provision to ensure best experience and outcomes for children. It is important to bring in evidence that supports your conclusions.

Now try this

Choose a research article of interest. Write a short paragraph that outlines the purpose and main conclusions. Show why the research issue is important for children and their families, supporting your points with examples from the research.

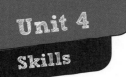
Research conclusions

Here are some examples of skills involved if showing how far secondary research sources support the conclusions drawn in a provided research piece.

Sample response extract

Other research has also explored the quality of pre-school provision relating to provision for outdoor physical activity. It found that there was variation between settings.

In this extract on research conclusions, a reference is made to other research findings but it is very general. You need to be **precise** about the findings and **cite the author** so that readers can find the research you are referring to.

Improved response extract

Other research conducted by Davy (2016) gathered information about early years outdoor provision to find how different settings meet the Early Years Foundation Stage requirements. The report, produced several years after Garrick, R. et al (2010), <u>Children's experiences of the Early Years Foundation Stage</u>, shows that there are still significant differences in the quality and availability of outdoor provision.

In this extract a reference is provided for the secondary source and it is **precise** about the research findings.

The differences in early years provision has also been explored by Sylva et al (2004). Although the study looked at the importance of pre-school in relation to non-attendance for improving outcomes for children, it also explored the 'value added' in relation to the quality of provision.

The learner cites an additional secondary source which gives **further support**, **validity and reliability** to their claims that the secondary research supports the conclusions of the provided research article.

Referencing your sources

Make sure that you reference your sources when you refer to them in your answers so your sources are clear to your readers and they can find the research you are referring to.

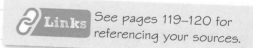 See pages 119–120 for referencing your sources.

Now try this

Find a secondary research source that is related to the issues in the Garrick, R. et al (2010) research article. You could use the source you found for the 'Now try this' on page 138. Write a short paragraph that outlines its purpose and main conclusions, and why the research is important for individuals. Explain how far this secondary source supports the conclusions drawn in the article.

Further research and methods

Here are some examples of skills involved if asked what you need to consider when planning further research with reference to a provided research piece and chosen secondary sources.

For example, if planning to carry out further research into the effectiveness of settings to support children's learning and well-being, further research methods and the ethics of the research would need to be considered.

Planning further research

Considerations for planning further research might include:

✓ **research methods** that could be used to continue research into the issue, **justifying** why they are **suitable**

✓ ensuring **ethical issues** are addressed, along with the **research skills** required and **practical** plans

✓ **supporting** any judgements made on **importance** of these considerations.

Sample response extract

For future research I would conduct research on the ways that the practitioners engage with children to find their learning and development needs. I would conduct observations and interviews with early years professionals and some children. I would also conduct some observations to see how children respond during play activities.

> In this extract, the learner states the methods they would use in their study but the **details** and **description** of their purpose are brief.

Improved response extract

For future research I would want to explore the ways that professionals engage with children to assess their learning and development needs. To do this I would need to conduct observations to see the strategies practitioners use. I would also obtain data from standardised assessments over a period of time so that I could measure children's progress. I would also conduct structured interviews with children to find their own views on their play, learning activities and learning progress. Through observing how practitioners engage with children in their play, learning and outcomes from assessment, I may understand how to improve my own practice.

> In this extract, the learner explains the type of research they would want to carry out.

> The learner **justifies** why they would use the methods of observation, interviews and assessment.

> The learner expands their response to provide a **rationale** as to why their future research will be **effective**.

Factors involved in further research

When planning to conduct a good piece of research, consider:

✓ the type of research you would undertake (e.g. the research title)

✓ the methods that could be used (e.g. triangulation of methods; ensuring reliability)

✓ the participants, how many and whether they will be randomly selected or not

✓ how this research is effective and suitable (e.g. does it build on previous research?)

✓ planning considerations (e.g. ethics, research skills)

✓ whether and how this will impact on early years practice and provision.

> **Links** See page 101 to revise factors involved in planning research.

Now try this

Using the research information from page 139 onwards, make notes of further research that could be planned into the issue of the effectiveness of settings to support children's learning and well-being. Justify the methods.

Further research and ethics

Here are some examples of skills involved if demonstrating understanding of the ethical issues that relate to research and the impact it will have.

Sample response extract

In planning this research one of the important things to look at is the ethical considerations. I need to make sure that I have been given permission to do the study and also that I have the consent of all the participants. For this I would need to tell them about the research I want to conduct, about their involvement and get their consent. I would need to make sure that I follow the ethical codes of conduct and any legislation that is relevant.

 This extract identifies the need to consider **ethical issues** related to the research but it is too brief.

The learner has identified that they need to follow **ethical codes** and any **legislation** relating to participants but they don't provide detail.

Improved response extract

In planning this research it is important to consider ethical considerations. Firstly, I need to ensure that I have permission from the settings that I can do my research. I also need to make sure that participants give informed consent, including parents of children. I have referred to the International Charter for Ethical Research Involving Children (ERIC) and the British Educational Research Association (BERA) code of ethics. I need to provide informed consent to all my participants and parents of children, telling them about my study and telling them their participation is voluntary and that they may withdraw their consent at any time. In research it is important that I adhere to legislation such as the Data Protection Act 1998 which tells me about how I can store and use participants' information. For example, I will keep all data in a locked filing cabinet or on a password-protected computer. All real names will be changed.

 This extract identifies the need to obtain **permission** from the settings where participants may be, alongside **informed consent** by participants.

 You should ensure that the children and their parents have the **mental capacity** to take part.

You should show that you have followed a recognised body's code of **ethical conduct**.

You need to show awareness of the **legislation** that governs **protection of personal data** and how you will **store** the information.

Research and ethical considerations

Ethical considerations are very important when planning research. You should:

- ✓ gain consent and access from the settings you want to conduct research in
- ✓ gain informed consent from centres/individual professionals, children and their parents
- ✓ consider mental capacity of participants/parents – can they make informed decisions on their own?
- ✓ consider any risk or harm to participants
- ✓ follow ethical codes of conduct
- ✓ comply with legal requirements including the Data Protection Act for participant data.

 Links See pages 108–112 to revise ethical considerations in research.

Now try this

Using the research information from page 139 onwards and the further planning guidance on page 145, make notes on the ethical considerations involved in your further research plans.

Further research and planning

Here are some examples of skills involved if planning and organising further research.

Sample response extract

To be able to carry out future research in this area I should make sure that I have taken account of the skills I need to conduct the research, and also be aware of any issues I might have in order to be able to complete the research in the time available. I need to set realistic timescales to complete the study and set deadlines for completing each aspect. I need to be able to find research literature quickly and be able to report it accurately. I need to apply an objective standpoint in my research.

 In this extract the learner has acknowledged the main **planning considerations** but needs to give more detail and examples.

 The learner has identified the importance of setting **realistic timescales** to complete the study.

 The learner has identified planning needs for **research literature**, **accurate** reporting and **an objective** standpoint.

Improved response extract

To be able to carry out future research in this area I would need to make sure that I have taken account of the skills I need to conduct the research and also be aware of any issues I might have in completing the research. For example, I need to ensure that I set realistic timescales that take account of illnesses, holidays, participant availability and other events that could delay my research. Research skills needed to explore this issue include being able to skim read literature; being able to analyse it and report it accurately and objectively using formal writing and referencing skills; possessing good formal writing skills that demonstrate a good awareness of the issue; and objectively discussing other literature to create a balanced argument. These and other skills help to ensure that I report literature accurately and am able to make more valid and reliable judgements that could have a positive impact on informing practice and provision.

 In this extract the learner has identified the need to **adhere to timescales** and qualifies this by giving examples of the **issues that can impact** on completing on time, so the plan is **realistic**.

 You need to identify correct **planning considerations** and give examples of **skills** you need to help create a **balanced argument** and produce a more **valid and reliable judgement** that will result in more positive outcomes for practice and provision.

Now try this

Review the skills needed to carry out the research you planned on pages 145–146. Make a list of any skills you would need to develop or provide, and how you would do this.

 Links See pages 101 and 133 to revise the skills you need in research.

Implications for practice and provision

Here are some examples of skills involved if focusing on implications of research in a provided research piece and chosen secondary research sources in relation to future provision and practice in early years.

For example, if the research issue is helping early years practitioners to improve effectiveness of their own pre-school settings to support children's learning and well being, you would need to consider the research conclusions and implications for how they might impact on future practice and provision in pre-school settings.

> ## Impact on practice and provision in early years
>
> When considering implications of the reviewed research:
>
> ✓ **analyse** and **explain** the impact on provision and practice for children
>
> ✓ **support** and **justify** any recommendations for change by giving reasons and examples.

Sample response extract

The issue I have researched has shown that there are differences in early years provision in different settings and this can affect children's experiences and outcomes (Garrick et al, 2010).

The quality of early years provision can vary and this will affect the outcomes for children as they reach Key Stage 1 (Sylva et al, 2004). These findings show that policy and staff qualifications can impact on provision.

Early years practitioners need to be aware of the views of children themselves to be able to plan for effective play and learning activities (Garrick et al, 2010). While most settings meet the requirements of the EYFS some still do not provide opportunities for outdoor play, which may impact on children's holistic development and well-being (Davy, 2016).

This extract starts with a reminder about the article to place the justification in context.

You need to provide an explanation of your findings and go on to provide detail of how this may affect individuals.

You should make reference to research. This helps to emphasise your understanding of the issue.

You need to include implications for practice and provision. This describes an implication for professionals who need to be aware of the views of children to be able to plan for their progress.

You should give good examples of how the quality of provision could directly impact on children's outcomes.

Now try this

Using the research within these skills pages, or related research that you identify, add a paragraph to the above answer. Give some good examples of implications for practice/provision, and highlight some of the positive outcomes.

You could include the benefits of involving children in assessing their own learning and planning for progress. You could show how this links to the principles of the EYFS and the implications for policy and practice.

Recommendations for practice and provision

Here are some examples of skills involved when making and justifying recommendations for future practice and provision in early years.

Sample response extract

The research findings show that working practices with children could be improved by taking their views into account when planning play and learning activities. This could be done by developing procedures for professionals to follow. Understanding provision from children's viewpoint will help practitioners to understand how children learn best, their interests, needs and the effectiveness of activities. Gaps in provision, such as outdoor play, can also be understood and identified.

Further studies could assess the success of responding to children's views, roll out strategies across different types of setting and update policy. The impact of research that explores children's experiences from their own viewpoint can be far-reaching. Listening to children can empower them to be involved in their own learning and development. This could have a knock-on effect for future curriculum guidance. It may help to promote greater collaboration across settings for the sharing of best practice, which can result in consistency in quality of provision.

 This extract from a response shows an understanding of how further research can be of benefit to future provision and practice.

 You should make recommendations for change, and support and justify them with reasons and examples.

 You should identify future research topics and how these might impact on practice/provision.

Implications for practice and provision

If focusing on the implications of research for practice and provision in early years:

 support your judgement by referring to examples from the provided piece of research and chosen secondary sources

 extend the discussion to consider implications of the research on practice (how the research might affect individuals in the workplace and day-to-day practice) and provision (the wider implications, including cost and effectiveness of service providers, and implications for society)

 make recommendations for change based on implications of the research for practice and provision, ensuring these are robust and reliable

 provide some rationale that backs up your explanation of the implications of the research for practice and provision within the early years sector.

Now try this

Using the research within these skills pages and your own sources, add a paragraph to the above answer that gives your own recommendations for provision and practice. Justify them with reasons and examples.

Answers

Unit 1 Children's Development

1. Growth
- head circumference
- length

2. Development
- 3–5 months old
- 6–12 months old
- 12–13 months old

3. Areas of development
Emma's emotional development

4. Holistic development
Language delay could impact on Joseph's:
- thought processes as he hasn't the language structure needed to think about, and express, his ideas
- ability to express his ideas and negotiate with friends in social play
- ability to express his emotions, which can cause frustration.

Other answers are possible.

5. Neurological development
Answers should include:
- The early years are the critical time for brain development.
- Interaction helps to make connections between neurons.

6. Atypical development
1 Specific delay
2 Examples may include:
   - difficulty in developing friendships
   - poor self-concept, so lowering self-esteem
   - affecting behaviour as it may cause feelings of frustration.

7. Genetic inheritance
Answers may include:
(a) Physical traits:
   - height
   - eye colour.
(b) Psychological traits:
   - artistic skill
   - disposition, such as confidence.

Other answers are possible.

8. Fine motor skills
Answers must relate to fine motor skills and may include:
- They will use a different type of grip. Connor uses a palmar grip and Amy holds a crayon between thumb and first two fingers.
- Connor will be able to pull on shoes but Amy will be more independent when dressing and be able to do up buttons.

9. Gross motor skills
Examples may include:
- They can join in with games that require physical skill.
- They can manipulate objects and toys to be able to join in with games.
- They can feel confident in their abilities.

Other examples are possible.

10. Maslow
The key person can:
- give Aimee a sense of security
- meet with Aimee's parents to discuss Aimee's physical needs
- provide Aimee with nutritious food and drink.

Other answers are possible.

11. Nature versus nurture
Positive effects may include:
- effective parenting supports and encourages children's learning
- good housing conditions with opportunities to play outdoors promote physical development.

Negative effects may include:
- a poor diet will affect growth
- poor housing conditions may affect children's ability to learn.

12. Societal systems
Examples may include:
- Meena will not have friends to play outside with so this will restrict her physical skill development.
- Meena's health and growth could be affected if the family cannot buy nutritious food.

13. Physical activities
Suggested activities could include:
- sit-on toys for development of leg muscles
- toys that move, e.g. balls or toy trains that are colourful and make noises, to encourage her to follow them.

14. Promoting development
Suggested activities may include:
- movement to an activity song
- ride-on toys around a track
- building a den from boxes.

Other correct answers involving gross motor or fine motor activities are possible.

15. Cognitive development
At Sami's age he should be able to:
- use ideas from his experiences in his painting
- use building blocks to build and make patterns
- talk about his experiences with sand and ask questions to develop concepts.

Other examples are possible.

16. Language and communication
(a) Micah is around 10 months old.
(b) Mia is around 3 years old.
(c) Bobby is around 7 months old.

17. Vygotsky
(a) Adults need to know the child's actual stage of speech, communication and language development so that they can identify the next stage that they are likely to be able to reach with support. This is Vygotsky's Zone of Proximal Development.
(b) Adults can then plan activities where they can support children to progress to the next stage.

18. Bruner
- The adult could encourage children to think about what the seeds need to grow, and extend thinking by asking them why.
- They could encourage deeper thought by speculating, e.g. 'I wonder what would happen if we put one pot on the windowsill inside and one outside'.

19. Piaget: schematic development
A schema is an idea or concept that a child develops.

20. Piaget's stages
a) Nathan is egocentric and will not be able to see things from other children's viewpoints.
b) Nathan will develop empathy at around the age of 7 years.

21. Information processing
Ellie will use her short-term memory to store information about her experience at the zoo.
She will recall what she has seen and apply it to her play.

22. Chomsky and Skinner
a) According to Chomsky's LAD theory, Saira has an innate ability to develop speech and language and will follow pre-determined stages.
b) Skinner's theory of reinforcement and repetition explains how Saira's speech and language skills will have been developed by adults around her repeating language that she could imitate and giving her positive feedback to her early language attempts, which would encourage further attempts.

23. Literacy
Answers could include:
Piaget: provide a range of books for Michael to explore so that he can construct his knowledge about reading.
Vygotsky: interact with Michael when he is looking at books, helping him to turn pages. Point out words that link to pictures, supporting him towards the Zone of Proximal Development.

24. Communication
Examples from own experiences may include:
use of Makaton to indicate snack time
eye contact/getting down to child's level
use of gestures/pointing.

25. Numeracy
The suggested activity could be one of:
- matching magnetic numerals
- using small-world toys such as farm animals to sort and count groups to five
- number dominos.
Links to theories may include:
- Helena's mother is scaffolding her learning by pointing out numbers in the environment (Bruner).
- Helena is interacting with her environment, which is helping her to construct her understanding of numbers (Piaget).
Links to other theories are possible.

26. Mathematical concepts
Resources may include:
buckets of different sizes, scoops and spoons
Bruner's scaffolding: the adult could model pouring a large container into a smaller one and smaller one into a larger one, asking 'What would happen if…?' to extend thinking.
Vygotsky's Zone of Proximal Development: the adult could support Nathan to sort shapes according to characteristics by asking him open-ended questions to get him to think about 'same' and 'different'.
Links could also be made to Piaget's theory of schematic development.

27. Exploring the environment
Piaget's schematic development: opportunities to explore technological resources will interest and enable children to construct their own learning/concepts.
Information processing theory: children will use their working memory to make the toys work, and may recall what they have learned when they next use similar toys to develop their play.

28. Emotional development
Answers could include:
- Jacob is unable to understand things from other children's viewpoint at his life stage.
- Jacob does not have the necessary language skills to express his needs or feelings.
Other answers that reflect Jacob's stage are possible.

29. Social development
Answers could include:
- Saeed will need to negotiate and cooperate with friends, which will help him to develop his speech and language.
- Having a close friend is likely to improve Saeed's self-image, which will lead to positive self-esteem.
Other answers are possible.

30. Behaviour: Bandura and Skinner
Own examples such as:
- pretending to use a telephone
- copying a dance move.

31. Bronfenbrenner
Own examples such as:
- a child's parent builds strong relationships with staff at the setting
- a parent shares a reading book that the child takes home
- parents discuss with the child what they have been doing during their day at the setting.

32. Attachment: Bowlby and Ainsworth
Because Ruby's mum is in tune with her needs there is a secure attachment between them. This means that Ruby is likely to be happy with the early years practitioners when her mother is still there but will show distress when her mother leaves. She will show pleasure when her mother returns.

33. Family systems
Answers could include:
- Support can be put into place to alleviate difficulties, which will reduce the long-term impact on children's holistic development.
- Insecurity is likely to impact on children's emotional and social development, resulting in them having difficulty in forming relationships.
- Children who are unloved/insecure may find more difficulty in coping with change/transition through their life.

34. Supporting relationships
Own example but could include:
Taking turns to talk about:
- friendships
- what makes children feel unhappy
- what children have done to help a friend
- discussing an incident/suggesting how to resolve a problem.

35. Stages of play
Own example but could include:
- play mat with road system, cars and small-world people
- outdoor sand pit with spades, buckets and dumper trucks.

36. Understanding self
Answers could include:
- Recognising the attachment style described by Ainsworth can help key persons to provide more effective support.
- Key persons work with parents to plan support so that there is consistency in approach at home and the setting.
- There should be expectations of behaviour appropriate to children's age and stage of development.
- Key persons should draw others' attention to children's behaviour where they have shown empathy and kindness in order to motivate them to repeat the behaviour.

37. Transitions

Answers could include:

1 Anjana may want to help with the baby and become more independent. She may feel left out, which could impact negatively on her self-image and self-esteem.
2 Anjana could help out with decorating the baby's room. Her parents could also read stories that explore the arrival of a new baby in the family in a positive way.

38. Early years theories

- Attachment is important for emotional development so having a named person in the early years setting makes the process of attachment easier (Bowlby's attachment theory).
- Working with the family to find out about a child's needs and experiences helps them to settle into the setting (Bronfenbrenner's bio-ecological systems theory).

Links to other theories are possible.

39. Your Unit 1 exam

Your notes on the Unit 1 exam, always referring to the latest Sample Assessment Material on the Pearson website for an indication of assessment details.

40. Short- and long-answer questions

Carly should:
- use simple sentences
- miss out linking words from her sentences, such as 'the'.

41. Responding to scenarios

A simple tripod grasp

42. Objective questions

- Aarif will develop self-esteem when learning new skills.
- Aarif will become more independent.

43. Scenario-based questions

- Because Helena has advanced language skills she will be able to express any problems and the way she feels, which will reduce the likelihood of her becoming frustrated.
- Helena will be able to use her language skills to build friendships. This means that she will feel good about herself, which will help her to develop self-identity and positive self-esteem.

44. Discuss and Assess questions

Delayed speech and language will impact on:
- Mia's ability to reason and express ideas
- the development of early reading and writing skills.

Other answers are possible.

45. Analyse questions

Answers might include:
Vygotsky and Bruner emphasised the importance of interaction with children in order to support their progression to the next level of understanding. Vygotsky observed that, with help, children could achieve at a level they could have not reached alone. He referred to this as the Zone of Proximal Development. Bruner, influenced by Vygotsky, recognised the importance of the role of the adult to engage or 'scaffold' children during active learning experiences. Each of these theories has implications for practice. Each theorist emphasised the importance of exploratory play for cognitive development but, unlike Piaget, Bruner and Vygotsky believed that children can be supported to progress and develop their higher order thinking skills. Continuous observation and assessment is therefore essential for planning for age/stage appropriate experiences, and by 'scaffolding' questioning and supporting children they can acquire new skills and understanding.

46. Evaluate questions

Answers might include the following:

(a) • Bandura's stages explain why children are motivated to copy the behaviour.
- The theory is based on his observations of children.
- Bandura recognised the importance of negative reinforcement to deter children from repeating unwanted behaviours.

(b) Strengths:
- Adults can change behaviours by modelling wanted behaviour.
- Negative reinforcement deters children from repeating unwanted behaviours.

Weaknesses:
- Extrinsic reinforcement is unlikely to be successful in the long term.
- Bandura did not recognise how behaviour can be influenced by genetic inheritance.

47. Applying theories

Answers might include:
The fact that Liam is following usual patterns of language development but still makes errors that are typical for this age group suggests that he has an innate ability for language acquisition. However, his experiences with books at home are likely to enhance his vocabulary and language use. This suggests a balance of nature and nurture in Liam's language acquisition.

48. Being concise

Answers might include:
Explanation 2: Because lifts are sometimes broken and the area is unsafe, Sadie and Marc will not have much opportunity to play outside. Lack of exercise will impact negatively on their gross motor skills, coordination and balance.

Unit 2 Development of Children's Communication, Literacy and Numeracy Skills

49. Communication

Examples may include:
- eye contact/getting down to the child's level
- pointing to an object/using gesture such as beckoning
- having an open stance/smiling
- showing an interest by paraphrasing/encouraging.

50. Language acquisition

Examples may include:
- pointing to indicate she wants a drink
- banging hands down to show frustration
- touching carer's face when she wants a cuddle
- raising both arms to be lifted.

51. Linked development

Answers may include:
1 role-play shop, game with turn taking, puppet play
2 Adults may:
- smile or praise children when they communicate, which according to Skinner will reward children so they repeat it
- expose children to language by modelling it, which according to Skinner is important for language development.

Other correct answers are possible.

52. Cognitive development

Examples may include:
- They can store information about their play and later recall their play experiences.

They can be given different resources that will help to extend their vocabulary.

They may use symbols to represent words in their drawings or in their play.

Other examples are possible.

53. Chomsky and Brown

According to Chomsky, children's language development will unfold naturally at a pre-determined time.

According to Brown, children will make mistakes in their sentence structure but this should be viewed as a natural progression through the stages.

54. Bruner

Answers may include:
- modelling language
- simplifying instructions
- using non-verbal gestures.

Other examples are possible.

55. Vygotsky

Ajay does not understand how to match the shapes to the holes in the posting box independently, but can do it with help from an adult.

This means that, according to Vygotsky, Ajay is in the Zone of Proximal Development.

56. Piaget

The children are in the pre-operational stage of development. They will not think logically but will use their senses to explore their environment and develop ideas/concepts about the characteristics of sand. They are using their actions to develop thought processes, which will help to promote their language development.

57. Factors affecting communication

The early years practitioner should make sure that the area is well lit and should face the child so that they can see their face. They should use gestures alongside words, use repetition and question to check understanding.

58. Observing and assessing

Examples may include:
- vocabulary and sentence structure
- use of non-verbal communication – eye contact, gestures
- listening skills and ability to respond appropriately
- how children follow instructions
- possible difficulties in hearing.

59. Babies and speech

Suggested activities:
- Hold Fariq and use a picture book, pointing to the pictures while saying the names clearly.
- Sit and face Fariq and use rhymes, such as 'Two little dickie birds' or 'Pat-a-cake'.

Other activities are possible.

60. Effective environments

Your own planning.

Characteristics may include:
- labelling of displays and storage boxes
- areas for quiet activities
- designated areas that encourage language such as puppet play or small-world toys
- role-play areas.

61. Promoting language

Your examples, but these may include:
- during an art activity
- during nappy changing
- story time.

62. Reading and writing skills

Your ideas, but these may include:
- Up to 1 year: feely/touch books
- 1 year up to 3 years: rhymes/traditional stories, e.g. 'Three little pigs', picture dominoes
- 4 years up to 5 years: computer software, word lotto.

Skills may include two from:
- handling books/turning pages
- understanding text moves from the top to the bottom of the page
- distinguishing between words and pictures
- linking sounds to symbols (letter shapes).

63. Language-rich environment

Characteristics may include:
- quiet and comfortable areas for reading and writing
- a wide range of reading materials
- a wide range of materials for mark making and writing
- labels that children can use/move
- labelled displays at children's eye level.

64. Phonemic awareness

Two activities such as:
alphabet puzzles, picture/word dominoes, picture/word bingo, computer software.

65. Reading development

Answer based on your choice of story or rhyme.
Literacy skills developed may include:
- recognising and joining in with rhyming words
- linking pictures with words
- recognising the shape of common words.

66. Literacy support

Story sack may include the story book, bear puppets or soft toys, different sized spoons and dishes, a packet of porridge.

67. Theoretical approaches

Your selections and reasons.

68. Reading sequence

1. Common words may include 10 from (or similar to): the, of, and, a, to, in, is, it, that, was, he, you, be, are, as.
2. Activities could include:
   - word bingo
   - word snap.

69. Choosing books

Your selections and reasons may include:
- 0–2 years: picture books that will encourage babies and very young children's interest in, and talk about, books
- 3–5 years: repetitive stories and rhymes that children will join in and learn to recognise and read words
- 6–8 years: more complex stories that will capture children's imagination, reflect their interests, help them to predict what happens next and to want to read independently.

70. Literary experiences

Examples may include:
- pointing out links between pictures and words
- demonstrating that text runs from left to right
- pointing out graphemes and linking to phonemes
- asking children to predict what might happen next.

71. Sharing books

Your ideas based on your choice of book or rhyme.
Skills used may include:
- stressing repetitive words
- encouraging/praising children when they join in
- using actions alongside words/rhymes.

72. Handwriting

Your observations.
Children may use:
- palmar grip, digital grip, simple tripod grip, tripod grip.

73. Writing development

Reasons may include:
- to develop a grip that will help children to write comfortably
- to develop control over the pencil to form letters clearly and at the correct height
- to give children confidence in writing down their ideas.

74. Writing sequence

Your ideas may include:
- writing in sand
- using large brushes on art walls
- finger painting.

75. Writing and reading

Your own ideas based on your story choice.
Resources may include:
- paints and writing materials
- puppets
- pictures relating to the story to colour and annotate
- story sequence with missing picture or words.

76. Literacy and home

Activities may include:
- Lend parents literacy games such as picture lotto to play at home.
- Invite parents to sit in at story time and demonstrate strategies to encourage Naomi to join in.
- Suggest book titles that Naomi will enjoy.

77. Mathematical experiences

Answers may include:
- measurement: heavy, light, full, empty, how much, more than
- shape and space: solid, flat, round, square, tall, short
- pattern recognition: same, different, what comes next.

78. Mathematical support

Answers may include:
- matching: coins, putting the same types of goods together
- pattern making: make patterns on 'pretend' biscuits to sell
- counting: counting number of bags for children to play with, counting coins
- sorting: sorting same coins together, sorting goods on shelves
- ordering: ordering coins in size
- recording: provide a notebook and pencil to record 'sales'
- sharing: sharing out resources.

79. Mathematical strategies

Your answer depending on your choice of rhyme.
You could use:
- 'Five little monkeys'
- 'One, two, three, four, five'
- 'One, two, buckle my shoe'.

80. Mathematical development

Your answer will depend on your choice of activity.

81. Supporting and assessing

Questions may include:
- How many cups of water will fit into the jug?
- What will happen if you pour the jug of water into the cup?
- Which container holds the most?

82. Mathematics and home

Answers could include:
- making number shapes with playdough
- ordering magnetic letters
- number jigsaws.

83. Multilingualism

Ideas may include:
- speaking simply and clearly
- showing photos or pictures alongside words to support routines (visual timetable)
- giving time in the day for the child to listen to a story in their home language.

84. Language learners

Ideas may include:
- display illustrations of the main routines during the day (visual timetable)
- arrange for an Arabic-speaking member of staff or parent to read a story in Ola's home language
- use gestures and positive facial expressions.

85. Additional needs

In speech and language delay, children are progressing in a usual sequence but more slowly than expected. In speech and language disorders, language development does not follow an expected pattern.

86. Supporting needs

You choose which signs to learn.

87. Professionals in partnership

Answers may include:
- to gather information about the child's background and needs
- to plan jointly for support
- to give advice and training on ways to support children.

88. Your Unit 2 set task

Your notes on the Unit 2 set task, always referring to the latest Sample Assessment Material on the Pearson website for an indication of assessment details.

89. Reading the brief

1 The brief introduces a fictional early years setting.
2 Thirty-four children attend the nursery. Around half are full time and others attend morning or afternoon sessions.
3 The nursery has;
- three rooms inside: baby room; toddler room; pre-school room
- an outside area.

4 Key issues to notice include three children whose home language is not English and four children

90. Making notes

- Skinner: operant conditioning. Children learn by being exposed to language; they repeat language when they are rewarded.
- Bruner: Language Acquisition Support System (LASS) explaining the role of social interaction with adults including parents for communication, speech and language (different view from Chomsky); adults scaffold language development by modelling and motivating.
- Piaget: cognition leads to language; exploratory play is important for cognition; different from Vygotsky and Bruner who say social interaction is more important.
- Roger Brown: stages of development that help to understand children's speech patterns/development.

1. Responding to case studies

You should not spend too much time on planning but it will help you to organise your thoughts. If planning a report, the outline plan should contain the main sections/headings, and information to include in each section. You could set out as a spider diagram as below.

Introduction –
reasons for report

2   Non-verbal communication –
examples of non-verbal communication
importance of non-verbal communication
best practice in use of non-verbal communication

Activities –
reading and writing
theoretical approaches

5   Conclusion/reasons for recommendation

4   Adult role in supporting reading and writing – ways to work with parents

2. Making recommendations

Example answer:

Children and even young babies can tell by your body language if you are interested in their communication. It is helpful to paraphrase or repeat back to children to let them know that you have both listened and understood. Asking follow-up questions encourages further speech. If your body language shows you are receptive, for example having an open stance and smiling, it indicates that you are receptive to children and encourages them to respond.

3. Justifying recommendations

Example answer:

If, as Piaget suggests, opportunities in the environment are important for children's speech, language and communication development, then the experiences in the home can be as critical as those in an early years setting. Vygotsky suggested that children can be supported to progress further by adults or other children who have higher level skills, which includes parents and older siblings in the home. This means that sharing ideas for activities and ways to support their children can help parents to provide effective experiences and resources.

4. Set of actions and activity plans

Actions could include:

- Encourage Timmy to copy consonant/vowel sounds: ma, ma, da, da.
- Use gesture when communicating with Timmy – pointing and waving.
- Play finger games with Timmy each day.

5. Recommending actions

Two more ideas for actions to support Elina's numeracy might include:

- Place magnetic numerals on a board and ask Elina to place them in order.
- Play a shopping game, labelling items with amounts up to 5p, and getting Elina to count out and pay with pennies.

6. Recommending activity plans

Completing activity plan 1 - example answer:

Environment
A carpeted and soft seating area in a quiet area of the setting.

Resources and equipment
Big story book that has a picture and related writing on each page. A stand to hold the big book.

Individual or additional needs
A child whose home language is not English.

Role of adult to support a child whose language is not English
Draw attention to pictures while saying each word.
Give time for the child to respond.

Use repetition and stress rhyming words.
Encourage the child to join in with others.
Arrange for someone who shares the child's home language to tell the story before the session.

97. Relating to theories

Example answer:

At the age of 3 years, children are not expected to 'read' the page but, by completing a rhyme or joining in with repetition alongside the adult, they are, according to Vygotsky, in the Zone of Proximal Development. Children will gradually begin to recognise words and have the confidence to read independently.

Unit 4: Enquiries into Current Research in Early Years Practice

98. Purpose of research

Example answer may be one of the following:
- What are the effects of music activities in the promotion of children's emotional well-being?
- Why do music activities promote children's emotional well-being?
- How can the provision of music activities help to reduce children's emotional distress?

Purpose: Improving practitioners' understanding of the importance of the provision of music activities for improving outcomes for children.

99. Issues in early years practice

Example answers:
- Provision: How working in partnership with parents and other professionals can improve outcomes for children.
- Early years pedagogy: The importance of a balance between adult-led and child-initiated activities.
- EYFS: Exploring strategies for reducing the risk of neglect and abuse.

100. Issues and the EYFS

Example answers:
- How well do early years settings meet the needs of individual children?
- What do practitioners understand by the 'unique child'?

101. Planning research

Example answers:
1   Triangulation means using different research methods to investigate the same research question from different angles. For example, using questionnaires, interviews and observations.
2   Triangulation increases validity of results by using several methods to achieve an answer.
3   Three things to consider when setting and monitoring realistic timescales:
    (a) Is the design of my study realistic? Will I achieve this in the time I have been given?
    (b) Are there any barriers to completing the study on time, for example holidays, work commitments?
    (c) If something is not working, will I have time to modify (change) it?

102. Rationale for research

Example answer:

Narrow/detailed issue: Lack of outdoor experiences for young children (a report on the DfE website suggests that there is wide variation in outdoor play opportunities for children up to 5 years).

Rationale: If practitioners are not aware of the benefits of outdoor play, it will impact the outcomes for children.

Research/working title: The impact of lack of outdoor play experiences on the holistic development of children.

103. Quantitative methods

Data that can be analysed statistically and that are measurable. It can be used to generate a hypothesis.

104. Qualitative methods

Example answers:

1   Qualitative methods are usually used to look **subjectively** at human behaviour and to interpret what children or their parents say about how they feel and experience things.
2   (a) Interviews can be used to find out what a parent thinks about an issue or an experience. For example, how confident are they to talk to an early years practitioner about concerns about their child?
    (b) Observations can be used to explore whether a child acts in the way you expect. For example, monitoring a child's interactions with others in a group over a number of sessions.

105. Advantages and disadvantages

Example answers:

1   One method could be to use a questionnaire to find out the strategies used by the key person to get to know the child and parent on entry to the setting.
2   One advantage of using questionnaires is that they can be used to gain information from a large number of parents quickly. A disadvantage could be that parents may misinterpret the questions or may not give accurate answers.

106. Research questions

(a) closed question
(b) closed question
(c) open question
(d) open question
(e) closed question
(f) closed question.

107. Target groups and samples

Example answers:

1   The children in the primary school.
2   (a) A stratified random sample. This means dividing the children into subsets or strata, e.g. boys and girls, and randomly selecting a proportional number of boys and girls for the sample.
    (b) A cluster sample could be used of just one class in the school.

108. Ethical principles

Example answers:

1   Three ethical principles are to maintain confidentiality, to obtain informed consent and to respect the human rights of participants.
2   The main purpose of an ethical code of conduct is to prevent any harm to participants who have consented (or children where parents give consent on their behalf) to take part in any research.

109. Safeguarding ethics

Example answers:

1   One key procedure researchers should follow under the Data Protection Act 1998 is to keep personal data stored in a locked cabinet or on a password-protected computer.
2   (a) Peer review (scrutiny of research findings by another expert in the field prior to publication).
    (b) Participant review, whereby people (or parents if participants are young children) who took part in the research are given the opportunity to comment and may ask that their data are excluded.

110. Confidentiality

1   participants' names and addresses, location of study, names of any organisations, identifying features

2   locations, names and other identifying features of organisations and settings, the names of any individual participants and gatekeepers

111. Informed consent

1   Informed consent means that the participant (and parent if the participant is a child) has been told everything they need to know to understand the project and has agreed to take par
2   It is important to gain informed consent so that participants are fully aware of what they are being asked to do and are able to make a judgement on whether they want to take part in the research; to ensure they are not likely to come to any harm.
3   Children should be helped to understand what is involved in the research using methods appropriate to their age and stage Their parent or legal carer must also give consent. Parents or other participants who do not have mental capacity to understand the project should have a responsible adult with them to give consent.

112. Legislation

Example answers:

1   Personal information must be (a) used fairly and lawfully (b) accurate and up to date.
2   One of:
    • Article 3: No person should be subjected to torture and inhuman or degrading treatment.
    • Article 8: All individuals have the right to respect of their private and family life, home and correspondence.
    • Article 9: All individuals have the right to freedom of thought, conscience and religion.
3   Answers might include:
    • Article 2: that children must not be discriminated against, whatever their background, status or ability.
    • Article 3: the best interests of children should be the primary concern
    • Article 12: children's views and opinions must be respected
    • Article 34: children must be protected from sexual exploitation

113. Non-judgemental practice

1   Taking an objective approach to research means that you keep an open mind to possible outcomes.
2   Bias means that you have already made up your mind about something. It can arise if you have pre-conceived ideas about what the answers to your research questions will be.

114. Primary and secondary research

Example answers:

1   Primary research gathers information that has not been collected before. Secondary research involves exploring and analysing existing data.
2   Two examples of primary research methods are observations and interviews.
    Two examples of secondary research methods are reviewing journal articles and analysing case studies.

115. Literature review

Example answers:

1   Secondary research examines both primary and secondary research about a topic. A secondary source is an interpretation of a primary source, so it is literature that has been written about that primary source.
2   The purpose of a literature review is to gain a deeper understanding of the topic and find out what has been researched before, to gain knowledge about primary and secondary sources and to evaluate how reliable each source is by understanding where each of the researchers has gathered their information from, to inform your research study.
3   A primary source could be a document giving a person's own original ideas or research or theory, for example Piaget talking about his work. A secondary source would be someone's interpretation of this original work.

16. Notes and records of sources

Your answer should include the following information about your piece of literature in a similar format:

Title	
Author	
Source and publisher	
Date of publication	
Page numbers	
URL and date accessed	
Key points e.g. research methods, key findings	
Connections with other sources of information	

17. Reading techniques

Skimming is running eyes over the whole text or article to get an overview of what it is about. Scanning is running eyes down the page to find key words to take in basic information. Skimming would be used to gain an overview of the content before deciding if it would be a suitable for own purposes so worth reading in more detail. Scanning would be used to quickly find a specific/key word or piece of information relevant to own research.

18. Academic reading and analysis

You should have found these sections in the article of your choice:

a) the abstract/introduction
b) the research methodologies
c) the results
d) the conclusions
e) the references/bibliography.

19. Referencing conventions

It is important to cite references correctly because:
- you should always acknowledge the source of any information to avoid plagiarism
- good referencing increases the validity of your work as it shows that other researchers have published supporting information
- readers should be able to access any source material that you used – good referencing will help them find your sources easily.

A **reference** section lists all the sources that have been cited in a text. A **bibliography** takes the same format as a reference list, but lists everything the writer read about the topic, not only the sources that are mentioned in the work.

20. Referencing techniques

Check your answer by comparing it with the examples given on page 120.

21. Selecting reliable research

Example answers:
Peer review means that experts have scrutinised and reviewed the articles before they have been published.
You would look at the date of the source. Research conducted in the past 10 years is usually classed as contemporary. Generalisations should only be made on the basis of large sample sizes that better replicate, for example the 'whole population' or 'all types of setting'. If the sample is too small the researcher cannot say that the results found would relate to the whole population.

22. Electronic searches

You should have found out how your library database works and have browsed the Association for Professional Development in Early Years website.

123. Connecting sources

Example answers:
1 Think about how the information fits into your own project and what information is still missing.
2 It is important to make connections between sources because this helps to result in a piece of research that is reliable and valid, and strengthens the argument or rationale for the research.

124. Suitability of sources

You should have used the SAMTAB approach and ethical principles checklist to assess a research article of your choice.

125. Interpreting quantitative data

1 Organising data.
2, 2, 4, 5, 6, 6, 7, 9, 9, 11, 11, 11, 12, 12, 14, 42.
2 42 could be an outlier.
3 Mean is 8; median is 9; mode is 11.

126. Interpreting graphs and tables

(a) $\frac{45}{250} \times 100 = 18\%$ (b) $\frac{7}{70} \times 100 = 10\%$

127. Bias in quantitative data

Example answers:
Leading question: Don't you agree that this government's policies on welfare reform are really making improvements to families in poverty?

Non-leading question: What do you think about the government's policies on welfare reform in improving outcomes for families in poverty?

A leading question such as this could influence the person being asked the question into giving answers that they think the researcher wants, in this case that the welfare reforms *are* improving practice and systems.

The effect of this research on wider policy or practice could result in practices and systems staying the same where, in fact, families may already be suffering as a result of current reforms, and no policies will be changed to reflect what is actually happening.

128. Interpreting qualitative data

Example answers:
1 Qualitative data look at what participants say and do, so means analysing words and actions/body language. Quantitative data deal with numbers so researchers look for meanings in numbers.
2 Research skills needed to analyse qualitative data include identifying common themes running through transcripts, deducing the meaning in the participants' responses and skim and scan reading.

129. Interpreting words

Your own response.

130. Bias in qualitative data

Example answers:
1 The researcher's body language can affect data collection. An open and relaxed questioner will receive different responses from someone who is tense and hurried, or aggressive, in their questioning. The respondent may feel intimidated and give the responses they think the researcher may want.
2 An example of respondent bias would be social desirability bias. This is when the respondent gives a response that they think will make them look good, so it may not be an accurate response.

131. Recommendations for practice

1 Current research provides information on the latest methods and their effectiveness, so helps to improve own knowledge and practice.

2 Answers could include subscriptions to professional journals (either own or through workplace), reading articles published by own professional body in magazines or on their website, keeping a log to record own learning and its impact on own practice, attending training courses, learning from other more experienced professionals in the workplace.

132. Recommendations for provision

Your own response.

133. Identifying future research

Answers could include:
- ways that early years setting collaborate on developing the key person role
- exploring parents' views on the benefits of the key person role
- the impact of the key person role on cognitive development
- children's experiences of the key person role.

134. Reflecting on research

Your own response.

135. Your Unit 4 set task

Your notes on the Unit 4 set task, always referring to the latest Sample Assessment Material on the Pearson website for an indication of assessment details.

136. Planning research

Your own response.

137. Finding sources

Your own response.

138. Making notes

Example answer:

1 The issue of early years provision is important because the quality of early experiences can have a profound effect on the outcomes for children. The research enables practitioners to examine their policy and practice from children's perspectives, which can bring about changes that result in children being placed at the centre of assessment and planning. As the government gradually increases 'free' hours for 3-year-olds and extends provision to 2-year-olds, the question of how well early years settings meet children's needs becomes more important. Disparities in practice are highlighted through research, which can lead to a greater understanding of EYFS requirements and sharing of best practice.

2 Answers will depend on the source selected.

139. Listing sources

Your own response.

140. Research methods

Your own response.

141. Suitability of methods

Your own response.

142. Methods and reliability

Example answer:

If you use several different research methods to research the same issue and they all give the same results and lead to the same conclusion this makes it more likely that the research results are reliable.

143. Research issues and significance

Your own response.

144. Research conclusions

Your own response.

145. Further research and methods

Example answer:

Future research could include:
- How far do practitioners involve children in their own assessment and planning?
- What are practitioners' views on the importance of outdoor play?
- Why do some children consider mathematical learning as 'work' but other areas of learning as 'play'?

Methods to be used could include:
- observations of practitioners: to find the strategies they use to engage with children in their play and learning
- assessment of children's learning and development at the beginning and end of the research period: this builds a reliable picture of the effectiveness of strategies used by practitioners
- interviews with children: although these may need to be adapted according to age/stage of development, including the use of pictures
- questionnaires and surveys with parents and professionals: if carefully constructed these can collect a large amount of information.
- All of these methods would be used in each setting for comparison purposes.
- Using a triangulation of methods will help identify any unreliable information.

146. Further research and ethics

Example answer:
- Gain consent and access from each setting.
- Gain informed consent from individual professionals, parents and other participants.
- Consider mental capacity of participants and, if they cannot make informed decisions on their own, ask a responsible adult to give consent and be present.
- Consider any risk or harm to children or other participants.
- Follow ethical codes of conduct.
- Comply with legal requirements including the Data Protection Act for participant data.

147. Further research and planning

Your own response.

148. Implications for practice and provision

Example answer:

This research will improve practice with young children. Practitioners will gain an understanding of the importance of engaging with children in their play and learning, including active physical play for positive outcomes. Research can highlight the effectiveness of strategies for involving children in assessment and planning so that training needs can be identified. This can lead to more focused planning that responds to, and better meets, the needs of individual children. The result would be the provision of an 'enabling environment' where practitioners 'respond to each child's emerging needs and interests' (EYFS, 2014).

149. Recommendations for practice and provision

Answers will depend on the sources used.

Notes

Notes

Notes

Notes

Notes